Funny Stories from Boy Scout Camp

Funny Stories from Boy Scout Camp

Seth Jaffe
Cover by Josephine Roberts
Illustrations by Valerie Vega

ISBN: 1511486244
ISBN 13: 9781511486248
Library of Congress Control Number: 2015904972
CreateSpace Independent Publishing Platform
North Charleston, South Carolina

I

My Introduction to Scouting

5 Things I truly believed would happen to mewhile working at Boy Scout Camp:

1.) I would rescue a princess from an impregnable fortress that was guarded by kids from my rival troop
2.) The Russians would finally invade America and my troop would have to hold them-off until the army arrived
3.) I would earn theArchery merit badge by shooting an arrow through another arrow on the bullseye just like Robin Hood (the cartoon fox version)
4.) I would earn Space Exploration merit badge after creating a rocket that successfully went from Earth to Mars and back.
5.) Girls would see me in my scout uniform and think, *Wow, I definitely need him to be my boyfriend!*

I wanted to be a Boy Scout ever since I was a little kid. Think about Ray Liotta in *Goodfellas* talking about how he wanted to be a gangster. That was me. All I wanted was to join the Scouts, and I knew it ever since I was five years old. No idea why, I just did.

Sitting in my room one morning, my dad walked in and asked if I wanted to go out for the day. For whatever reason, I looked at him and asked if it was for the Scouts. He smiled and said, "Let's go." Lo and behold, it was. We went to an official Cub Scout pancake breakfast. Starchy Bisquick with synthetic blueberries was the meal that began my love of scouting—that along with seeing the soldiers of the Webelo Army walk by in unison, resplendent in all their blue uniformed glory.

A few months later, I was enrolled, and just like that, I was in scouting. I breezed through Cub Scouts, earning Bobcat, Wolf Bear, and then Webelo. Now it was time for my varsity call-up. I was going to the big show: the Boy Scouts of America. I enrolled in a local troop in west LA and then it was on to my first backpacking trip to Sespe Creek in the southern California mountains. The adult leaders, my dad included, dropped off the cars, and it was a few hours of backpacking before we would hit the campsite. I walked along in silence, mostly listening to the older scouts talk about girls, fireworks, previous camping trips, and, most importantly, girls. The more they talked about girls, the more one thought kept floating through my mind: it would be so great if we could play Capture the Flag tonight.

Finally, in the late afternoon, we arrived at our campsite. It was perfect. There were ledges, rocks, and more places to hide than in the Ewok village on the Forest Moon of Endor. There was literally no better place in the world for a bunch of scouts to spend the weekend. The second we dropped our gear, a guy in his late twenties and a woman of about the same age came up to talk to us. Their names were Bob and Susan, and it turned out they had just gotten married that morning. Tonight they were on their honeymoon, and they specifically reserved our campsite for its isolated location. Oh my God! This was their honeymoon, and they were going to share their campsite with twenty Boy Scouts. *They were so lucky!*!! They could play Capture the Flag with us. (I wanted Bob on my team, not Susan. It's a scientific fact that girls aren't as good as boys at Capture the Flag.)

Our new friends could cook s'mores and help on our snipe hunt. How happy were they going to be? After the newlyweds had a brief discussion with our scoutmasters (Bob probably had some ideas about Capture the Flag strategy), our leaders made an executive decision. We would hike down to the next campsite, away from Bob and Susan.

Our next campsite was hardly as exciting as the Ewok village more likely a suburban housing tract on Luke's home planet of Tatooine. Regardless, we dropped off our gear and started to explore. Approaching the creek bed next to camp with anticipation, I caught a frog, tracking him down like I was a highly skilled hunter in the wild or Arnold Schwarzenegger in Commando, knowing full well that bad guys could be smelled if they were upwind. I brandished my amphibious conquest for all my fellow scouts to behold. And then it happened—Eric, the wise-and-mighty teenager and leader of the elder council, spoke up.

"You guys know if you stick a pin up a frog's butt, it will explode."

"What?! No way! Really?!"

Eric was fifteen. He wouldn't lie. Plus he had a job that required top-level security clearance: he operated the candy store at the park. He absolutely would know something like this. He was the smartest person I knew. And he sold Red Vines. And they were awesome!

The idea snowballed.

"Well, you need a pin."

Drew, one of the other younger scouts and a first-time backpacker like myself, chimed in. "Yeah. Hey! I've got one in the sewing kit my mom gave me."

Eric's friend, Steve, our resident troop bully, responded. "Ha, Ha. Your mom made you bring a sewing kit, you loser."

I don't know about you, but I love bullies.

The great enigma that pre-dated the Mayans was about to be solved. Would a pin up a frog's butt make him explode? Something that I discovered only five minutes before was now the mystery I had waited my whole life to answer.

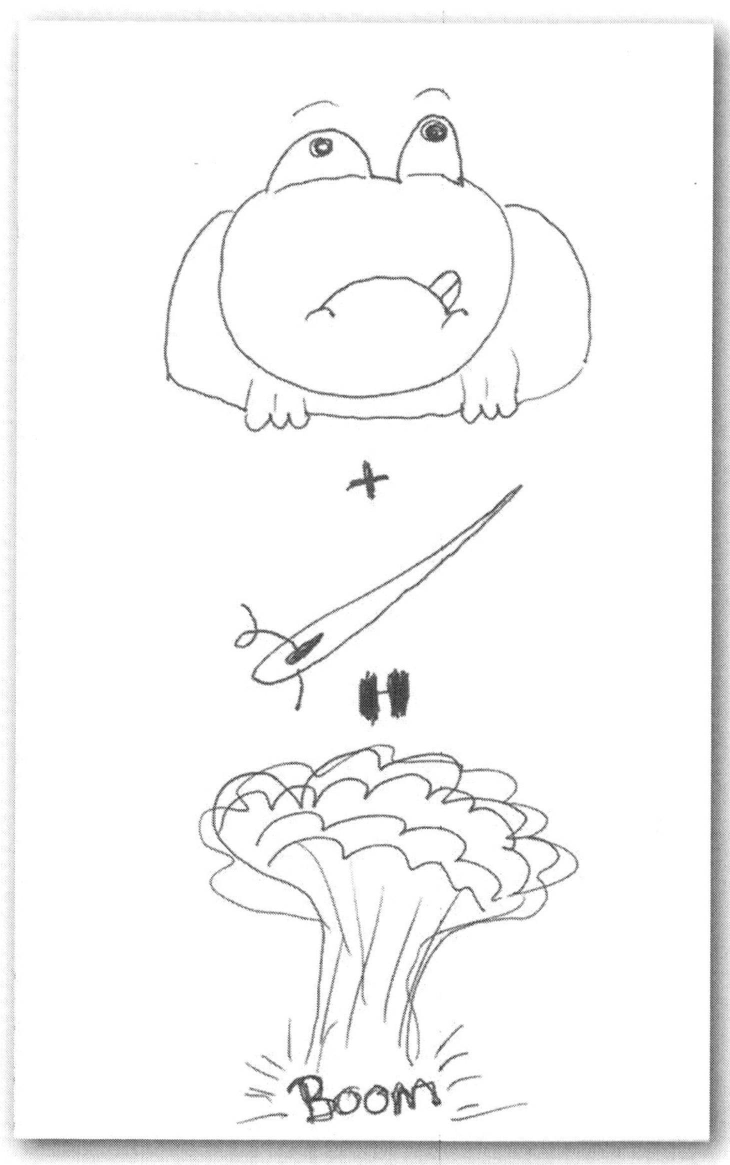
BOOM

I stood by, breathless. Eric, our fearless leader, held the frog in one hand and the pin in the other. The two hands drew closer together. My eyeballs glared intently forward and narrowed in focus. Looking back on this one moment, it was the greatest focus I have ever displayed in my entire life. I paid less attention during midterms, finals, driving, playing sports, and my wedding day combined.

I looked left. I looked right. Pin/frog/pin/frog/pin/frog—and suddenly, *Bam!*

As the pin drew closer to the frog, he somehow got away. Surrounded by pre-teens and our teen ombudsman, the frog somehow escaped Eric's grasp and was able to make a jump for it. He made it past the little rocks and then into the water. The great mystery of a pin up a frog's butt leading to a cataclysmic explosion was never answered. But to this day, I know it's true because Eric claimed it was true, and he probably had a girlfriend, and he also sold red fruit punch in the little plastic bottles, and did I mention he was a genius?

Looking back, it's obvious what happened. Eric, fearing for my personal safety, let the frog go to avoid an explosion along the lines of the Fukushima Nuclear power plant. For that gesture, I will always be grateful to him. With the failed frog weapons test concluded, I decided to explore some more.

Soon enough, I found a way to ruin the goodwill from catching a frog and have everybody in camp turn on me. When I say everybody, I mean *everybody*. They all yelled at me—the other scouts, the scoutmasters, and my dad—all because I decided to go to the bathroom within one hundred yards of the creek.

Steve, the bully, went first with his usual subtle critique: "You idiot. You're retarded."

Then my good friend, Jake, chimed in. Jake and I went way back to Cub Scouts. He wouldn't be that mad at me. I bought him an Atari game for his birthday. We were good friends.

> "You just ruined our water supply, you moron," he said. "We're all gonna get sick. Dysentery kills kids every day. I hope you're happy."

I could see the report on the evening news: "Fifteen scouts from Troop 171 were all pronounced dead from a severe strain of malaria that was caused by one scout who went to the bathroom less than three hundred feet from the water supply."

But before I could respond in kind for my indefensible transgression, something magical happened. A gust of wind descended on Sespe Creek.

For thirty seconds, we were in a bona fide windstorm—dust and sand everywhere, and then a flying tent. All this windstorm was lacking was a giant sandworm from the movie *Dune* to steer us to safety. We watched as the tent flew into the air and descended forty feet up on the branches and directly over the water. It was my scoutmasters' tent. The wind had taken hold of it and lofted it into the trees where it was now stuck. There was only one solution.

The rock solution.
Eric turned to us.

"Gentlemen, get your rocks ready."

For the next twelve hours, we stoned that tent like it was an infidel in a small Pakistani village.

> "Death to the heretic Jansport who is a nonbeliever in the coming of windstorms to Sespe Creek!"

Finally, after the tent had taken enough brutal punishment for her scandalous behavior and she still wasn't coming down from the branches, our scoutmasters told us it was time to pack up our things and leave. I can only assume my scoutmaster's tent is still hanging there to this very day, twisting in the wind, serving as a cautionary tale to other scouters to please put in their tent stakes before they do anything else.

II

The First Week Working at Camp

The 5 best movies involving buried treasure:

1.) *Treasure Island*
2.) *Raiders of the Lost Ark*
3.) *Goonies*
4.) *Pirates of the Caribbean: The Curse of the Black Pearl*
5.) *King Solomons Mines*

The greatest scouting experiences I ever had occurred during the summers I worked at Camp Emerald Bay on Catalina Island. This is not a story about being a model Boy Scout. This is a story about a bunch of kids who worked at a scout camp. These are my memories, filled with all of the nonsense, idiotic behavior, and alcohol-induced mayhem that made the summers spent on Catalina Island the most fun I ever had in scouting, if not in my whole life.

—∽∽—

My very first week at Emerald Bay was in the summer of 1992. I worked in the nature area. This was probably done because anywhere else meant real responsibility. In the nature area, there was no access to guns, bows and arrows, or even the ocean. No kids were drowning on my watch, not in the middle of benches and trees. They kept me in the summer camp equivalent of a padded room. It was a series of outdoor classrooms in the trees. Gymboree is the Death Racc of England by comparison.

At the end of my first week on staff, it was merit badge-testin' time. This is when all the scouts come in to pass a rinky-dink test and go back with a souvenir merit badge to make their parents happy. In no way, shape, or form should this be the equivalent of South-Korean-high-school-placement-test day. To reiterate, you should never see a headline from freemalaysia.com that reads, "Exam Pressure Drives Teens to Suicide."

Enter the scoutmaster.

I looked him over. He looked a little ragged, but nothing out of the ordinary. Also his shirt and shorts were wet. His troop must have just returned from their war canoe trip. The War Canoe Trip was where a troop loaded up all of their scouts and scoutmasters into canoes and sent them a few miles away from camp to an isolated area called Parsons Beach. While there, the kids canoed some more, snorkeled, and cooked hamburgers. As part of my job as an official "Nature Scoutcraft Ranger I not only taught classes, but I was also entrusted to lead war canoe expeditions on a weekly basis as well.

The scoutmaster walked up to me.

"My kids are in your class."

"OK."

"There're six kids from our troop."

"OK."

"We were on our War Canoe trip."

"OK."

"And I left my shoes on the beach."

"OK."

"Their Ritalin was in my shoes."

"Uh-huh…" (I always knew the right thing to say in the presence of adults.)

The prescription-drug craze was just getting started in the early nineties. The notion that you pill-pop a kid into submission was in its infancy. You knew about Ritalin because somebody had a cousin somewhere who was using it, and it kept him in line. Plus I think that on Season 3 of *The Real World*, Pedro suggested Puck needed help (read: Ritalin) after he stuck his fingers in the peanut butter.

Enter the very stressed children. Time for my big speech to show the kids that I cared.

> "Hey, guys, gonna be a little merit-badge test today, but it's cool 'cause if you don't pass, instructor Seth is totally gonna help."
>
> "What? No! We're not ready. We didn't study. *WE DIDN'T STUDY*!"
>
> What do you mean 'if we don't pass'?" The kids continued. "Are we gonna fail? We can't fail. *WE CAN'T FAIL*!" (Failure was not an option.)

Pictures of the South Korean students entered my mind. I could see it now: My students were going to climb to the top of a Catalina cherry tree and jump ten feet to their deaths because they didn't get their camping merit badges. (It is, after all, required to earn your Eagle.) Or worse yet, and maybe this was just my imagination running wild, but maybe they were all going to climb to the top of a one-hundred-foot tree above the ocean and jump to their deaths in a pit full of sharks while they lit themselves on fire and shot arrows at one another on the way down.

Why did you fail us?
Now we'll never get Eagle

I envisioned the courtroom scene:

> "Seth Jaffe, you stand before this court charged with six counts of letting Boy Scouts self-immolate themselves while jumping off a cliff [a solid two hundred feet now, not one hundred] with rocks tied to their shoes, plummeting them to the depths of the safe-swim area [fifteen feet]. All this because they lost out on getting the one badge they needed, nay, the one badge that was required for them to get their Eagle. How do you plead?"
>
> "OK."
>
> "Further, you stood by and did nothing, knowing full well that any other badge they earned at camp, sans environmental science or first aid, was meaningless in comparison to this required badge. How do you plead?"
>
> "OK, I mean, guilty."

At that moment, with the rest of my life flashing before my eyes, I knew I needed to rally the troops. It was time for a great speech from a great speaker to calm the seething masses. I summoned Churchill, Roosevelt, and MLK for one moment of verbal amazement.

> "You know what? We won't call this test a test, but let's take it anyway. It'll be fun."

Gandhi would have been proud.

After the test was over, nobody was dead. Our pass rate was slightly better than the UT football team's graduation rate. Hook 'em Horns! Good enough for me.

My last vivid memorythat stood out from my first week working on staff was simply called "Orange Boy." A scout taught me this skill, which I have no doubt was taught to him by previous scouts all the way back in time to the very first ancient scouts who chiseled Orange Boy next to Osiris and Anubis in the pyramid city of Hamunaptra. Here is what Orange Boy looks like (big budget on my first book).

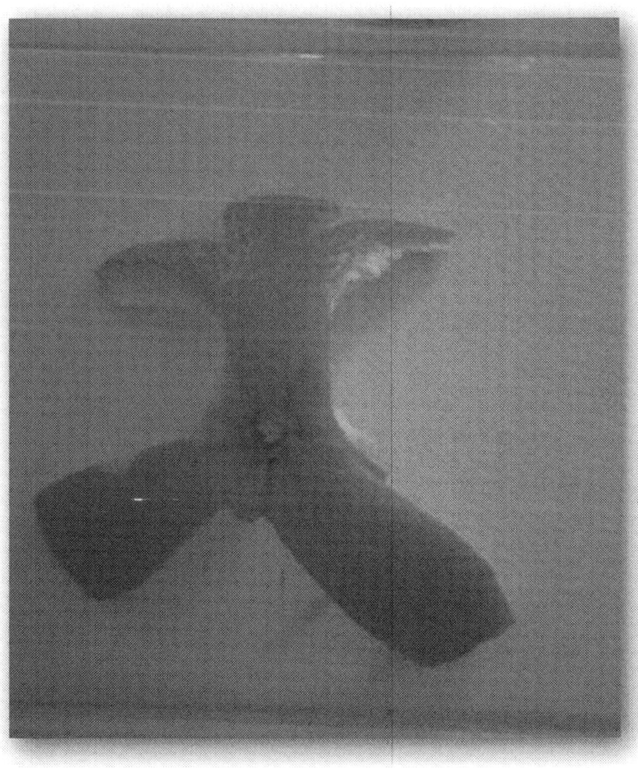

Got me laid exactly zero times in college…I was counting.

III

Carvillak's Speech, or, as I Like to Call It, the "Get Some Pussy" Speech to Chase and Sam

Five Greatest Summer Camp Movies of All Time:

1.) Addams Family Values
2.) Meatballs
3.) Ernest Goes to Camp
4.) Friday the 13th
5.) *The Parent Trap* (original version)

—∞—

The chapter title says it all. I rate this speech in the pantheon of the greatest speeches I've ever heard. Not of all time, mind you, but just where I have personally borne witness. Again, it ain't George Washington talking about needing glasses because his eyes sustained some wear and tear fighting for our independence, but it ain't bad.

Now me personally, when I think of great speeches, I think of one of my favorite movies of all time: *Any Given Sunday*, starring Al Pacino, Jamie Foxx as Steamin' Willie Beamin', and, most importantly, Jesse Spano from *Saved by the Bell* (and *Showgirls*...that movie was also awesome).

As I was saying, I rate this speech up there with Al Pacino as the coach in *Any Given Sunday*, telling the team before the playoff game, "The inches we need are everywhere around us." I mean, it's up there with Steamin' Willie Beamin' in *Any Given Sunday* going toe to toe with Pacino and saying, "I put the points on the board," and, of course, it's up there with Bill Bellamy to LL Cool J in *Any Given Sunday* with the groupie sluts in the room, saying, "Word yo, this bitch was tellin' me my sausage wasn't right." Such a great movie. Anyway, here's the setup for this one fuckin' awesome speech.

(Disclaimer: The names have been changed to protect the stupid.)

Most of the kids at camp didn't look like me. They didn't have back hair, or a receding hairline, or the imposing physical demeanor of a guy who can bench press thirty-two pounds (with a spotter). Most of the guys looked like they were taken straight out of a weekly yachting magazine. Two of those prime examples of purebred royals were Chase and Sam. These guys actually knew how to talk to girls. Chase and Sam met some yachtees' daughters one day while hanging out at the waterfront. This happens at a summer camp.

Boats come in for the weekend, and while Mom and Dad are luxuriating on the stern of their boat sipping chablis, their teenage daughters sally forth in the family dinghy to cruise the bay. Our staff members would hop into a motorboat and venture out in search of girls. Upon meeting them, you would find a rendezvous point for some sweet Island Lovin'. This never worked for me, but it actually happened for, I don't know, every other guy who worked with me. All my buddies could pull a Marlon Brando and find some island tail. I always had to import, and, for the record, that shit didn't happen until way later anyway. My virginity was still safely intact, circa 1992.

Chase and Sam met some girls during the day, and they were sneaking out to meet them on the beach across from camp later that night.

This is standard operating procedure when you work at an island summer camp. The rules are pretty elementary: Find your lady friend. Arrange a meeting time and place. Also make sure you don't tell anybody. One other pointer was to sneak out for your rendezvous after the 10:30 p.m. curfew. And again, let me also stress the whole point of *don't tell another fucking soul where you're going or what you're doing.*

Carvillak was one of the senior staff members. Initially he and I did not get along at all. This was in part because of the political stance I took against working hard to set up the camp the week before the kids arrived. We eventually became great friends, but our initial meeting was rocky. Also Carvillak was in a tough spot. It was his first year as a Director, and they made him responsible for the Handicraft area. In the nature area, nobody ever got injured. Plus it was quiet and relaxing. In the handicraft area, you were surrounded by kids who hit mallets into metal disks for their metalwork merit badges.

All you would heard was *Clank, clank, clank!*

Clank, clank, clank!

All day, incessantly, from 9:00 a.m. until 8:00 p.m.

The other popular badge there was wood carving. To earn this badge, a scout had to carve a small neckerchief slide, typically a crow or a dime-store Indian. I'm sure it's a little more politically sensitive now, not the (untrademarked) Washington Redskins mascot.

The only time the pounding or the carving stopped was when a kid missed his intended target and hit his finger. This meant that you had kids whining about finger cuts and bruised thumbs multiple times per hour. I personally tried to earn the wood-carving merit badge, but after ten minutes and two finger slices, I quit that badge and never looked back.

When my friend Tommy was in the Handicraft area years later, he made the kids who sliced their fingers sign the wall of blood. They wrote their names on a plaque and then placed the bloody digit next to their signature as sort of an official seal. Tommy got the list up into the seventies, and he was only at camp for two weeks that summer.

On a side note, the greatest scam I ever saw perpetuated at camp occurred years later when a kid working the handicraft area named Kareem informed his students that if they wanted to get their leatherworking/metalwork/wood-carving merit badges, they needed to march over to the trading post and get him a Coke and a candy bar.

What a brilliant scheme. This kid became the Michael Milken of junkfood bonds. Unfortunately, like all great con artists, our Bernie Madoff Jr. got greedy and let a perfectly good con get wildly out of control. Instead of Kareem just telling the kids to hang out in the handicraft area, he got them to bring him his Mr. Pibb and M&Ms and then he sent them on their way. Once they showed up in camp with a merit badge that was supposed to take them a whole week to earn and not forty-five minutes, the scoutmasters became livid and immediately notified the camp director. You can do a lot of things at summer camp, but the second you let the kids out early and the scoutmasters have to actually deal with the kids directly, you can expect some sort of punishment. This kid's fate was sealed. Plus, like all great Ponzi schemes, Kareem kept telling his students to bring in their friends so they, too, could get merit badges in exchange for an orange soda and a Three Musketeers. Kareem was fired before the first week of camp was over. The trading post never saw such glorious profits, except, of course, years later when they hired a girl with huge boobs. Then their stock shot up like the Google IPO.

Carvillak was surrounded by kids all day banging mallets onto metal and slicing their fingers incessantly. While his friends played in the ocean or went on hikes through Catalina, he sat there and listened to the same noises over and over again.

Clank, clank, clank!Clank, Clank, Clank!

He probably needed an outlet for all the anger that was building inside of him. That outlet was Chase and Sam.

Somewhere there was an inside man. Or a leak. Carvillak knew what Chase and Sam weredoing and where they were going. Ironically though, Carvillak didn't even want to catch these kids, let alone walk half a mile out of his way to their secret-lovin' rendezvous point. All he wanted to do was look into the cabins, check off the kids as present and accounted for, and then go to bed. That's all bedcheck is anyway: making sure the kids are in their bunks and then calling it a night and going to bed yourself. Carvillak even had the courtesy to flash his flashlight like he was a tour guide and walk loudly in hopes that Chase and Sam would hide from him. During the Vietnam War, I don't recall Charlie ever doing that to lost jet pilots in the Mekong Delta, did he? I mean, that is one nice fucking gesture to make. Details are fuzzy, but the important thing is these morons didn't hide, and of course they were caught.

I was awake in my bunk (not masturbating, by the way, thank you very much—more on that later), and I heard footsteps. Justice was being delivered back to the cabin of the captured. Total silence. You could hear a tissue drop…or a page turn (again, *NOT MASTURBATING*, PEOPLE!). Then the ass-chewing heard 'round North Hill began. Carvillak opened fire:

> "So, Chase and Sam went to the other side of the Camp to get some pussy!I guess you guys didn't

> think you might actually get fucking caught; that's how stupid you were. Well, good for you two, except it didn't work. *I* SWEAR TO FUCKING GOD, CHASE AND SAM, YOU TWO HAVE TO BE THE BIGGEST IDIOTS ON THE ENTIRE FUCKING ISLAND."

Then he imitated their voices, doing a surprisingly good impression of Chase and Sam, kind of like in *Animal House* during Bluto's "Nothing is Over" speech when he says, "Oh, we're afraid to go with you, Bluto. We might get in trouble."

Carvillak mimicked Chase and Sam, saying, "Oh, we thought we we're going to meet some girls. Oh, we're so smart. NO YOU'RE NOT! *NOW GO TO FUCKING BED*!"

Breathless, heart racing. I was just happy it wasn't me. Then the cabins all started to whisper amongst themselves, like prisoners in a Viet Cong tiger box. (Except for the guys who got away because the Viet Cong were courteous enough to make a lot of noise while they were on patrol.)

Viet Cong number one: "I have to leave my rice paddy this weekend for my sister's wedding in Da Nang."

Viet Cong number two: "Will it be typical Ao Dai or the more elaborate Au Menh Phu?"

Anyway, let's leave the magic of the Dark Cell Tiger cage and journey to another time, after the speech apocalypto:

My cabin and every other cabin were all talking amongst ourselves"That was fucking awesome."

"Holy shit, they're in trouble."

"Oh my God. Hey, we should shut up and go to bed. I don't want to get yelled at, especially by Carvillak."

"Don't worry. He's long gone. No way he can hear us."

From a distance:

"SHUT THE FUCK UP AND GO TO BED, JUNIOR STAFF. GOD DAMN IT, I CAN HEAR EVERY WORD YOU GUYS ARE SAYING!"

IV

The Savoy Salad Bar and the Great Escape

Five Best Movies that Involve Scouting:

1.) *Indiana Jones and the Last Crusade*
2.) *Up*
3.) *Troop Beverly Hills*
4.) *The Last Boy Scout*
5.) *Moonrise Kingdom*
6.) *Honorable Mention: Destroy All Planets**

*I never saw this movie, but how could it not be included, based upon the Wikipedia description listed below:(Gamera vs. Viras) (1968) At a world scout jamboree in Tokyo, two young scouts get mixed up in Gamera's battle with world-conquering aliens."
That sounds so awesome!

—~—

My first year on staff, I learned about the fine correlation between being good-looking and getting away with ineptitude on the job. This will shock you, but I learned that sometimes good-looking people can get away with subpar work. One of the rangers on staff was a kid named Rick Munstatt. Physically he was everything that I was not—blond hair, blue eyes, and separate-but-equal eyebrows. They don't make 'em like that at Hebrew School, let me tell you. Shockingly Rick was popular with the ladies, and that gave him major street cred at camp. He was also an atrocious worker. Rick was straddling the median point between an A- on one side of the spectrum and a solid F at the other end. And you don't pass with F's.

Tonight, Hallmark Channel presents a very special after-school movie:

You Don't Pass with F's.

(Starring Kristen Stewart as the unruly teenager and Meredith Baxter-Birney as the out-of-touch mom.)

Rick's ineptitude led me into trouble my first week at camp. Rick and I were assigned to take a few troops on their War Canoe Trip to Parsons Beach. We would be supervising four troops comprised of approximately eight scoutmasters and sixty kids.

The initial departure from camp went smoothly. Even the landing wasn't catastrophic. Nothing more than a splash of saltwater on the scouts. Totally forgivable transgression. Rick was helping me, and it felt like the beginning of a functional working relationship.

Then it turned.

The first thing Rick did when we got to the beach was commandeer a few canoes so he could take some scouts to an abandoned area on the side of a cliff called Smuggler's Cove. The cove was basically a hole in the side of a cliff where you could sneak in a couple of canoes and then there was a cave-like rocky beach. The rumor was that National Geographic had sent in a team to look for lost pirate treasure in the seventies, but after finding a doubloon and a sword, they gave up. (I know it's a stupid rumor and you're asking right now why they gave up, but come on! I was seventeen, and we were literally inside the cove when I was told this story. It made sense at the time.) Also you had to go into Smuggler's Cove at low tide, otherwise you either

a.) couldn't get out;

or

b.) would get thrashed around the rocks

or

c.) would find more doubloons, and sabres, and pistols than you would know what to do with, and then you'd probably overload your canoe with all of your magical pirate treasures.

Some of the staff, myself included, had paddled there during our camp setup week before the scouts arrived. We were given a very clear-cut speech by the Ranger Director just before we entered:

"Never, *ever* take kids here. Also, don't ever go here in high tide. Lastly, do not, I repeat, do not let these canoes get banged up against the rocks. Use yourselves as human shields if you have to because I don't care what happens to you guys because junior staff are worthless. But do not, under any circumstances, let the canoes get harmed."

OK. Got it. The canoes are worth more than our lives. No problemo. It's not like I was smart enough to tell high tide from low tide anyway. I just figured there was never a reason for me to ever go to the cove.

Well, Rick was off. The four canoes full of small scouts, mostly younger kids, were heading to Smuggler's Cove to go look for lost pirate treasure. Once you commit to a treasure hunt with a bunch of kids, they ain't backing down.

I waited. Then the rain came. Given that I've only seen rain twice in my entire time spent at the island, you could say it was something of an anomaly. I sat on the beach at my first war canoe trip without any other staff—just me and a bunch of scouts and scoutmasters alone in the rain.

I wrangled up some kids for a game of thirty-on-thirty touch football, but after forty minutes of this, the kids were bored and the scoutmasters were wet, tired, and complaining. To be fair, the scoutmasters were always complaining, but now they were wet and tired as well.

From the corner of my eye, I saw four canoes approaching. They were paddling really fast. When they pulled back onto the beach, I discovered why they were in such a hurry. Rick had taken in all four canoes at once during what was apparently a high tide.

Smuggler's Cove was basically a small tunnel that connected the ocean to a hole in a cliff. Two of the canoes dipped down as they entered the cove and then the tide came in fast. As the water level picked up and filled the tunnel, the canoes went straight up, and a bunch of scouts hit their backs against the top of the entrance.

(At least nothing bad happened to the canoes. Thank God.)

With a slew of kids piling out of canoes, covered in scratches and bleeding on their backs and the tops of their heads, it was time for the first-aid kit. Hooray.

At least Rick would help me. I would be like Hawkeye from the MASH 4077th, and he could be Pierce. Nope, Rick had other ideas.

Like an absentee dad trying to get out of his court-appointed custody visit, he conveniently ignored the kids he injured and went to get a new group of healthy kids.

Rick asked, "Who wants to play some football?"

As I applied gauze pads on a scout's back, I told Rick, "Yeah, dude, I just played football with the kids and they're kind of burnt out. They might not want to."

The scouts immediately responded,

"Awesome idea, Rick. Let's play football. Rick is the best, huh guys?"

"Yeah, we love Rick."

Chants cascaded, "Football with Rick! Football with Rick!"

Weekend dad was running laps around full-custody stepdad.

I watched as the magnificent-and-wonderful Rick led the kids in a much better game of thirty-on-thirty football.

Soon after, Rick got bored. This happens when you're good-looking and dumb. He turned to me.

> "Hey, Seth. I'm going to walk to camp and get something. I'll be right back. You can cover for a few minutes, right?"
>
> "Sure, Rick. No problem."

It was my very first week at camp. Rick was my War Canoe buddy. If he was Ice Man, then I was Maverick. No way was I gonna let him down. Of course, he was leaving his position, not me, but that's not the point.

The rain continued…

An hour passed…

Still more rain…

One of the scoutmasters turned to me and announced that his troop was walking back. They didn't want to be stuck on a beach in this rain.

I didn't know what to do. It was my first War Canoe Trip. Should I make them stay? Should I go get help?

The rain continued.

Two hours later, Rick came back. Turns out he did find what he was looking for back in camp. He was looking for a nap.

The rain continued for another hour. Then it began to lessen, but morale didn't improve as the nozzle switched from heavy drizzle mode to mist.

Eventually Rick and I helped light a campfire, and we had dinner.

The next morning, we loaded up our gear and went back to camp.

I figured everything was good. We left with a few troops, and they all came back—except, of course, for the one troop that walked back in the rain and left all their paddles and camp supplies at the beach.

Immediately the second I got out of my canoe and set foot on camp soil, the Waterfront Director as well as my Ranger Director started in on me. The interrogations continued from every member of the senior staff who was present. I was called up to this de facto board of review like Captain Kirk after he crashed the Enterprise.

> "*SETH*! Why the hell did you let a troop walk back to camp? They left buddy tags at the waterfront. Those buddy tags weren't claimed. For all we know, they could have drowned."

A buddy tag was a small paper marker that a kid left at the waterfront to indicate if he was canoeing, row boating, snorkeling, etc. This way we knew where he was if he needed to be found. But I digress. Back to the yelling… at me.

> "Seth, this is serious. What if those kids were drowning right now?"

I wondered how two scoutmasters and ten kids could drown if they were walking on a hiking trail.

(Better table that question for another day.)

"Also, why did your troop leave their canoes and paddles back at camp? Now we have to go get everything. And what were you guys doing over there? I've heard a lot of complaints. Didn't you take them on any hikes or exploring in the snorkel areas?"

(Hell, no! Rick abandoned me, and I didn't know what the hell to do because nobody trained me.)

I'm a lot of things, but I'm not a snitch. I did the only thing I could think of in this situation.

"Sorry, guys. Won't happen again."

I thought it was over until later that night when it was time to go to sleep. *OK* I thought to myself. *I'm safely in my cabin. I'm exhausted and I just want to go to…*

"Seth Jaffe and Rick Munstatt. Get down here now! I swear to God."

It was Lomas. He was a tall, angry black man, and you did not want to get on his bad side.

Lomas was our maintenance man. His voice was booming, and I'm convinced that when he yelled loud enough, the shock waves that rippled through the air broke the wings off of Angels. It's unsubstantiated, but I stand by my theory.

"Seth and Rick. *GET DOWN HERE NOW!*"

We both walked down.

I spoke first (because I'm an idiot).

"Hey, uh, Lomas. What's up? Is everything OK?"

"No, it is not OK! The God damn scouts you took to Parsons Beach messed up the latrines, and I ain't cleaning it up. You both are! Let's go now!"

We took the van of despair over the trail to the camp. Then Lomas handed us mops and buckets. If you want to know what I looked like mopping, picture Prince Akeem in *Coming to America,* mopping with the mop still in the bucket. I lacked a lot of life skills when I was seventeen.

Rick and I sat there and cleaned up the latrines for forty-five minutes.

—∿∿—

Later on in the summer as I actually became a better—or at least more functional staff member (moving from that C+ category into solid B- territory), Rick became abysmally worse. He was constantly late, was caught drinking—hell, he even threw buckets of water on some of the Senior Directors while they were sleeping, including Carvillak, the guy we all feared. This was a big no-no at camp. Much like Joe Pesci run amok in *Casino*, the bosses had had enough.

As the summer neared an end, we knew Rick was on borrowed time. He had no allies left in camp. It was just a question of time. I, on the other hand, had improved. I was now a good staff person. Some of the senior staff and alumni who visited from time-to-time even said they hoped they saw me back on staff next year. Yipee!

All of our cabins had different hotel names. My first year, I was in the Royal Hawaiian. There was also the Biltmore, the Kona Kai, and the Ritz. Rick Munstatt lived in the Savoy.

I was in my cabin one night getting ready for bed. From where I was, I could look down on some of the other cabins below me, and I had a perfect vantage point of the Savoy.

I saw four directors walk up to Rick's cabin. Each one of them held something in his hand. I couldn't tell what it was, but I was transfixed.

The door opened slowly. Then it hit me. Rick was in that cabin. Holy shit. I'd seen *Full Metal Jacket* I don't know, about fifty times. It was required viewing if you were a teenage boy. It made Vietnam seem like so much fun.

It was time for a beating party. Soap bars inside of towels. I crouched down and braced myself. Any second now the screams would start.

And then nothing.

Nothing at all.

Total quiet.

In fact, the door opened, and the four directors walked out of the cabin. I looked into their hands. Each one of them seemed to be holding a dispenser of some kind. Almost like the ones in the kitchen.

A minute later, the door to the Savoy opened again.

I was staring at a ghost.

A figure that almost resembled a human form walked out of the cabin.

He was pure white. I had never seen a ghost before. Best not talk for fear of the ghost noticing you. Then my nose picked up a scent. It was subtle at first, but then it grew stronger.

Ranch dressing.

I looked closely. Rick was covered in Hidden Valley. He looked like a cross between Casper the Friendly Ghost and a contract girl from the valley working with Lexington Steele. Bacon bits were falling off of his arms like he was shedding. You couldn't see his actual arms and legs. Only oil slick marks where Thousand Island and syrup had been placed.

Rick walked straight to the shower, dripping a trail of actual bread crumbs along the way.

This is exactly what Rick looked like when he exited his cabin.

SAVOY

—⁓—

But it wasn't over. The directors still wanted another piece of this guy. That's how much they had grown to hate him, and around mid-August, it was known Rick was leaving.

The general rule of thumb for camp staff when you left the island (and it doesn't appear to be very scientific) is they throw you in the water. (Ironically, in my later years, we only threw the kids in the water we liked. If you didn't get tossed, you knew you weren't really welcome back.) Getting tossed in the drink wasn't a big deal. In fact, it was more a badge of honor. It was the staff's way of saying that we like you and we want you to stay a part of this family.

I figured when my time was up, I would just walk up there and wear the shirt and scout shorts that needed to be washed the most. Wet staff socks, wet Tevas. Not a big deal at all. In fact, I sort of appreciated the camaraderie of the whole situation.

But I knew they had bigger plans for Rick. I had no idea what, but I was not going to miss out. Rick's exit date was the second Saturday of August. Other staff members were leaving as well, not just Rick. This included Sam, the poor guy (read: imbecile) who was apprehended before his quest to get a sweet, innocent, naïve yachtee's daughter to give him a hummer on the beach was realized. Sam didn't agree with my theory that you should wear your dirtiest clothes for the boat ride home. Quite the opposite, in fact—he opted for a different outfit on his ride home. Sam decided he wanted to look his best for the boat ride in case some sexy ladies were on board. Not factoring in that he could wear dirty clothing and get a free ocean laundry cycle, Sam wore custom jeans, a top-flight T-shirt, and his brand-new, perfectly pressed staff jacket that somehow had made it through the summer unscathed. In Sam's eyes, sometimes there were girls on the cattle barge home who you could talk to for a solid forty-five minutes, and that meant looking your best. Boy, he looked sharp. As he walked down the docks, I thought to myself, "Wow, saltwater is really going to mess up that outfit."

Within seconds of hitting the final dock station, Sam was greeted by the senior staff, who wished him an emotional and tearful farewell by pushing him into the water.

Splash!

Sam climbed back up on the dock, livid and screaming.

> "What the fuck is this? You can't push me into the water! I don't fucking like this, and my outfit is ruined!"

All this went on while scouts were walking by to get on the boat.

One of the directors walked up. "Hey, Sam, cool off."

Whoosh!

Back into the drink for Sam. I totally thought that would happen. Still it was awesome to see.

Meanwhile, no Rick.

We waited.

All the scouts boarded.

All the scoutmasters boarded.

The last members of staff who were leaving got on the boat.

Still no Rick…

He had to be in camp. We had all watched. Hell, the senior staff told us that if we saw Rick to let them know. The line on to the boat was watched more closely than any prisoner segment of the Bataan Death March. Nobody was unaccounted for.

Suddenly a loud noise came from the boat. I watched in awe. There he was safely on board, There was Rick.

> "You all thought you could catch me. I got away. I outsmarted you all."

The assistant waterfront director yelled back,

"That's OK, Rick. You won't ever be invited back anyway."

It was the last we ever saw of him at camp.

Lateron that day, I was trying to figure out what happened. Turns out, one guy on staff saw what Rick did to sneak on the boat and chose not to say anything. Maybe he was protecting Rick. Maybe he was protecting the senior staff from themselves. After all, what was the point in going after a guy who was never coming back to camp anyway? I watched the assistant waterfront director, furious that Rick got away, proceed to whack a canoe paddle against the ramp in anger until it snapped. *Probably good that Rick got away*, I thought to myself.

Either way, Rick's escape plan was brilliant. Here's how it went down: He packed all his gear, then instead of taking all his gear onto the boat himself, Rick gave different pieces of luggage to different troops and asked them to carry everything for him. Staff luggage stood out because it was much larger than regular scout luggage. We were there for two months. They were there for seven days. We would've seen Rick walking down the docks with two months' worth of luggage. Unless, of course, he asked a few troops to carry his gear onto the boat for him.

That was all fine and good, but how did Rick actually get on board? Turns out he wasn't as dumb as he acted. In a pinch, the guy could actually pull it together. Rick put on a regular Boy Scout hat he got from the lost and found and a pair of dark aviator sunglasses. Thenhe paid kid five dollars to lend him his scouting shirt. He made sure to find a kid with either a medium or large shirt (I'm guessing) with the rank of Second Class on the shirt. Anything higher, and he might have been flagged. While his luggage went on in separate bundles, Rick went on a few minutes later, blending in as Joe Scout from Troop 654. As much as I didn't like the guy, I had to hand it to him—it was an amazing exit strategy.

V

The Great Burgee Heist of 1999

Five Eagle Scouts We Can All Be Proud Of:

1.) Neil Armstrong
2.) Gerald Ford
3.) Mark Madsen (greatest Laker championship parade speaker of all time: "Thank you!")
4.) Jim Mora ("Playoffs!")
5.) Steven Spielberg

Our camp was and still is surrounded by weekend yachtees. They descended on the bay every summer like Russian paratroopers from the opening scene of *Red Dawn*.

> "Now the great hunt for open moorings would always begin with weekend boaters in a semicircle."

There was a yacht club to the right-hand side as you faced away from camp, as well as numerous yacht clubs using open areas throughout the island. Each yacht club had their own burgee for identification purposes. A burgee was a gigantic flag that identified the specific yacht club that was there that weekend. A burgee, to these people, was like the liberal eugenics genotype markings from the movie *Gattaca,* but much more pretentious and self-righteous.

The greatest source of pride known to mankind if you worked on staff, was to steal your very own burgee. Again, island street cred could be attained at a price, and that price was a yachtee's burgee. In 1999, it was my last song and dance at the island. I was leaving my gig at scout camp for the glamorous world of selling insurance. Toward the end of the summer, the yachtee bourgeoisie had positioned themselves for an evening party. It was their last big hurrah, which made it my last big hurrah. Almost everyone had a stake in getting that burgee.

Among my friends, I was starting to feel like the last man standing.

Clint already had a burgee. Clint was a former track star in high school, and even though his daily diet consisted of orange soda and trading-post candy, he could still play any sport in spectacular fashion. He also had a deep appreciation of the history of both scouting as well as Catalina Island. For him, stealing a burgee was about historical significance, sort of like punching your ticket to an antiyachtee hall of fame. Clint obtained his burgee one night while a few of us walked back from our beloved Isthmus Bar. It was up there on a flagpole and he simply lowered it down. The high-school track star did the least athletic feat imaginable to get his burgee. It was sad really, sort of like Mitch Richmond riding the bench with the Lakers to get his only ring.

McBrayer had his own burgee as well. McBrayer was a botanical sciences major at Cal State–Hayward. He was a supreme athlete much like Clint. He mountain biked, rock climbed, kayaked, and was, generally speaking, a freakishly badass individual. He also became stronger with more alcohol, sort of like Godzilla in stormy weather. McBrayer also liked having sex with psychotic women, but that's neither here nor there.

Late one night, after alcohol turned on the ignition of McBrayer's courage switch, he swam out to a boat and used their dinghy to climb up and snake a burgee off the bow of a boat while the yachtees were blissfully asleep inside. McBrayer's burgee theft had every tacit skill I lacked. He went across cold open water, at night while lacking the necessary sobriety. We're talking *Act of Valor* here, but much more heroic. Those real-life marines weren't three fingers deep into boxed wine when they saved their target. To not have a burgee was not an option for me. I needed an easier out, and the end-of-the-summer yachtee party was it for me.

I looked out at her during the day while I planned. There she was, blowing in the wind just begging me to steal her, taunting me with her curled monogrammed embroidery and ostentatious insignia. This burgee was a blood diamond made from the blood, sweat, and tears of hedge-fund managers who had to sacrifice one weekend a year in the Hamptons. Otherwise how else was there going to be a second regatta of the August sailing season? I wasn't just doing this for me, or for the eight-year-old children in Jakarta who stitched her together (Nice work, Ramelan and LingTang. Tell Budi to stitch harder next time!). Again I... was... doing... this... for... me!

And to brag to my friends.
And for Immortality!
"Strength and honor."
"*AS ONE*!!!!"

With my master plan in my head, I needed to kill some time. Plus, I needed to be seen with my buddies so that I could have an alibi. Clint, Allen, Jake, and a slew of directors all congregated in one of the small cabins to pass around some Franzia and listen to Busta Rhymes's *Extinction Level Event*. We knew how to wine taste. All I had to do was stay long enough so that nobody suspected me. Plus if I kept drinking (which I was totally doing), people would assume I was too drunk to steal anything as high priority as a burgee. We passed the box of merlot around while Busta serenaded us with chants of, "What the fuck you want."

I was drunk but not as bad as the rest of the crew. Clint was about to pass out, as was his roommate, Allen. Allen was a burly badass who would go on and become an EMT for the city of San Diego. That guy could outhustle me for a burgee any day of the week. Fortunately, he'd been drinking, and that made him lazier than a DMV employee on a Friday at

4:40 p.m. before Memorial Day weekend. Still, Nilius was the worst. Nilius was a six-foot-four chiseled Adonis who had a forty-inch vertical and more game with the ladies than Shawn Kemp in his baby-making days. Nilius was also an engineer with a huge nerd side to him. This guy got mad if his girlfriend confused *Star Wars* with *Empire.* Asking this guy about Jar-Jar was like asking ISIS for their views on gay marriage. His engineering geekdom was always running at critical mass. It's probably why we liked him so much. Nilius drank and drank. The guy looked like he was about to toss his cookies at any moment. I'm no expert, but this might have had something to do with the fact that, in between gulps of boxed wine, Nilius downed his very own concoction. He would mix Gatorade with tequila. He even coined his own term for this drink: the Gatorita*tm. The guy was absolutely obliterated. He started to stand up and grabbed at his stomach.

We all yelled in unison:

"Whoa, whoa, buddy! Not in here! No way!"

The last thing we needed was for that guy to get sick and throw up. Not that I was going to help with the clean up.

Nilius started to stagger out of the cabin and fell into the side door.

"You need help, buddy?"

"No, dude. I think I got it..."

We watched him barely make it in the general direction of his cabin.

The dominoes were falling. Everybody else was passed out. It was almost go time.

At eleven that nightp.m. (well past normal drinking and masturbating time), I left. With my buddy Jake in tow, we proceeded on our long walk (half a mile). Down through camp, hook a quick right (or starboard, as they say in fancy boat speak), and we descended on the leftover Yachtee's party. Simple enough plan: Do our quick recon for food and alcohol (preferably alcohol) and then we haul their flag on down. Gentlemen, let the heist begin.

Jake and I arrived in total silence. This was so easy. I couldn't believe our luck. We walked up to the flagpole and undid the ropes so we could lower the burgee down into our open arms. We got down there, looked up and *Poof!* She was gone. Our burgee was not there. We were too late. There was a feeling of utter shock and amazement that two lazy drunks were outthought either by the yachtees or the younger, more sober members of the staff. No burgee for us to steal.

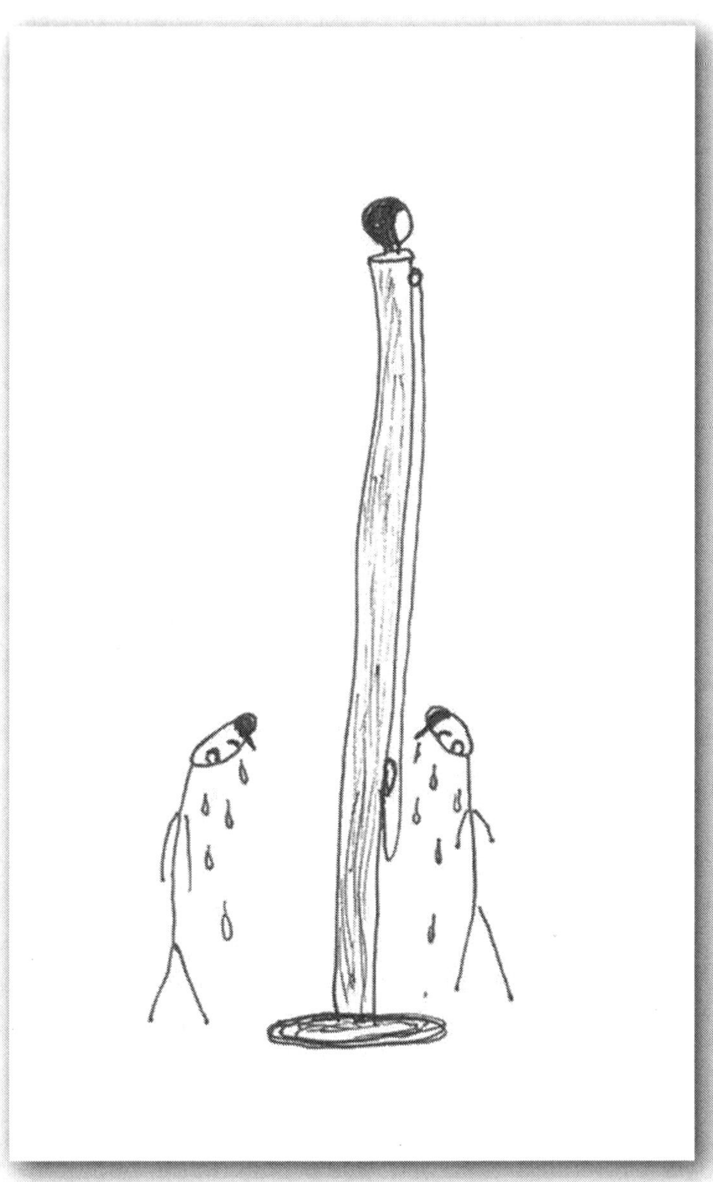

Jake turned to me and said, "What do you want to do now, Seth?"

> "I don't know, dude, drink…or I guess…we… could…ahm, keep on walking for a while to the other yacht clubs and see if they have a burgee."
>
> "OK."

There were now two of us on this quest, a quest that had taken us from the front of camp to the full distance of half a mile. Our quest continued to the fiery depths of Mordor. Unfortunately our path was beset with some rocks that sometimes got inside your Tevas, which was incredibly painful. Our never-ending journey (fifteen minutes and counting) moved forward. So endlessly we trekked…a full mile from camp, past two more yacht clubs. We trolled for burgees like they were fat girls at a bar just before 2:00 a.m. closing. Our window was about to slam shut, and we were desperate. Sadly, no burgee…not on this day. Our journey was at its end, so we made the U-turn. Our quest for the precious had failed. Almost three whole miles of walking, and we had nothing to show for our efforts.

The next morning our business director came up to my A-frame. This was a pleasant surprise. I never got visitors in my neck of the woods. I always had to walk from the nature area into camp to see people. Hell, John Walker Lindh gets more visitors at Supermax than I ever did working in the backcountry.

"Hey, Derek, what's up?"

"Seth, did you steal the burgee?"

"Excuse me, Derek, what?"

"The yacht club president is over, and he's pretty upset. Did you steal their burgee?"

"No, Derek." (Ironically, I didn't sound that convincing at this moment. Maybe I just wanted to experience the feeling of being a master criminal, nay a "Smooth Criminal" Da Da Dadada!)

Derek continued. "Well, the president of the yacht club is talking to the camp director, and he's pretty pissed. Now granted, he knows it was pretty stupid to leave it up last night for someone to steal."

***Ooh, I loved this strategy. Blame the victim. Blame the victim. This works all the time on Lifetime Movie Network and whenever there's a rape trial in Orange County. Make her feel guilty for letting her hot, slutty burgee dangle in the wind, taunting us, the innocent children of hedge-fund managers and county sheriffs.

"Seth, we think you stole the burgee. Can we search your stuff?"

They actually knew it was me. There was a tear in my eye; I was so flattered. Now I had to let them down and end this charade.

"Derek, I went down there last night [pause for effect] so I could steal the burgee. [Another pause...

this time for dramatic effect.] And when I got there, it was already gone. The point is this, Derek: I am as mad as you. I want to know who stole this burgee because they beat me there. I went a whole summer without stealing a burgee, and somebody cost me my title shot."

"OK, Seth, never mind."

"No, Derek! You find out who did this, because I am furious. The nerve of somebody else to take something that was rightfully mine to steal."

"Good-bye, Seth."

"Avenge me, Derek! Avenge me, Derek!"

This was the greatest alibi in the history of time. This alibi was so good, I was a lock. No way was I guilty. Plus I was actually innocent here, but that's not the point.

"If the burgee does not fit, you must acquit."

They never found the Lindbergh burgee.

—ɱ—

Three months later I was in Tucson, Arizona, to watch the USC–Arizona game. More specifically, I was there because I had a sure thing, and I knew I would be gettin' some. I felt like Flounder in *Animal House.*

"I hope I score tonight, oh boy!"

Since the plan to "get some" backfired, which was a shocker to nobody except for me, I now had to focus on drinking, as well as on a football game between two particularly shitty Pac-10 football teams that year. Disclaimer: Now only one is shitty, and the other is coming off of probation because they allowed impermissible benefits to be given to Reggie Bush's family by a runner for an agent as part of their win-at-all-costs mentality. For Shame! Also, it's the Pac-12 now.

I was, for all intensive purposes, off the "Dingo ate my burgee" case, kind of like Special Agent Johnny Utah from *Point Break*. Now, here I was in Australia, still looking for Bodhi before he catches his last wave in the fifty-year storm.

> "Look at it! It's a once-in-a-lifetime opportunity, man! Let me go out there and let me get one burgee, just one burgee before you take me in. I mean, come on, man, where am I gonna go? The one law enforcement officer on Catalina on both sides! I'm not gonna paddle my way to San Pedro! Come on, compadre, come on!"

I digress. From out of the corner of my eye, a slow-moving pickup truck rolled up, honking alongside a screaming, nonsensical driver.

Classy words cascaded through the desert landscape. "Yeah, bitchez!" followed by the ubiquitous, "Check this shit out!" I looked, and there he was: Nilius.

Very closely It all came together.

On his dashboard was my burgee—the burgee I never had a chance to steal. The burgee that was never accounted for despite all the cell tossing and searches that were conducted at camp. He'd had it this entire time. We never thought it was Nilius because we saw the guy get face-down drunk the night before and pass out. Or did we?

Nilius couldn't have done this, could he? I thought back. That night he drank with us. No big shocker there. Then he left early to go to bed. He was staggering around, so there was no way that he was sober enough to attempt to do something of this magnitude. Unless, of course, he left early and deliberately faked being drunk so that we wouldn't view him as a threat. Then he would have had more than enough time to race over to the flagpole at the yacht club and hoist down the golden prize.

I felt like Chazz Palminteri in *The Usual Suspects,* solving a case as the lead suspect left police headquarters.

> "The greatest trick that the devil ever pulled was convincing everyone that he was just a big dumb waterfront goon who drank Gatorade and tequila. [It's called a Gatorita*tm, people.] And like that...he's gone."

To this day Nilius's burgee is still in his condo garage museum. It sits alongside such priceless works of art as Microanoscale Science textbooks and a can of WD-40.

VI

The *Seinfeld* Bet

The Five Most Awesome Badass Eagle Scouts Ever:

1.) Albert Belle ("Joey! Joey!"...oh, the fun I had at Yankee Stadium.)
2.) John Heder ("Gosh!")
3.) Clive Cussler (Am I the only person who liked the movie *Sahara*?)
4.) John Tesh (I even met him at a Boy Scout camp once.)
5.) Shane Victorino (The Flyin' Hawaiian)

Our favorite show on the island was *The Simpsons.* By decree you loved *The Simpsons,* and if you didn't, that meant the penalty of death to the infidel. After *The Simpsons*, we enjoyed us some *Seinfeld.*

We were all walking one day when I spoke up.

"It would be funny, guys."

Allen responded, "What would be funny?"

"You know, that episode of *Seinfeld*...the one with the bet?"

"What bet?"

"What are you? Dumb? The masturbation bet. We should do the masturbation bet and see who lasts the longest."

Allen at this point fired back, downright angry at me.

"Are you fucking stupid, Jaffe? You won't last three seconds. There's no way you can win."

"No, no, guys. I'm totally serious. We do the bet. Everybody puts in like five dollars. Allen, or Clint, or somebody can hold onto the cash, and we'll do honor code."

"Well what are the rules?"

Now we're talking. A little competition here. Gotta get those competitive juices flowing, or in this case, not flowing.

"Welp, let's see. You gotta come clean if you beat-off" (such a nineties phrase...so much worse than the classier contemporary counterpart of "launch my groin goblins").

"Also, if you have sex, gay sex in your case, Clint, 'cause you're gay, then that doesn't count, and you're still in the bet." *Disclaimer: Clint's not gay. He's just the one black guy I know who has a copy of Natalie Merchant's *Tigerlily*. (By the way, for those of you curious about my stance on gays in scouting, just read the next sentence: *LET 'EM IN ALREADY*! *WHAT'S THE BIG FUCKING DEAL*?!!!)

The having-sex rule was actually a terrible idea, and here's why. I made a rule that did nothing whatsoever to assist me, while basically helping every other person involved. Let's just turn the ball over on downs because we want to be nice today.

Back to the game at hand, or in this case, Oh Nevermind!.

"Everybody good here?"

Collective yeah. "We're good."

Details are fuzzy, but as I recall, I think there was a token "Whoa, Bundy" afterward in honor of our third favorite show, *Married with Children*. Ironically we couldn't watch this show during the duration of the contest since the idea was not to masturbate. Sorry, Christina Applegate, you would have to wait. Again, details are fuzzy, but I'm pretty sure that up until this point, I had spent a good portion of my summer I don't know, masturbating to Christina Applegate. And Baywatch. I loved Baywatch.

Noon (Cue the *Law & Order* music!)

"OK, so it's cool. Everybody is good. No worries. I can win this. This bet is easy. Just hold out a few days and score some action at the Isthmus. Not a problem. Not at all."

5:00 p.m.

"OK, this was a stupid idea. I hate this. You guys are all awful. Each and everybody sucks except for me. I hate it here!"

6:00 p.m.

"When is dinner?! This is fucking bullshit. When is fucking dinner? I am starving and these Goddamn scouts get to eat first. What the hell is that?! I work at this camp and what the hell do they do, for Christ's sake! I give them their mammal study merit badge, and this is how they repay me? WTF! What's for dinner tonight anyway? It better not suck, I swear to God!"

7:00 p.m.

"What are you looking at?"

The war of attrition was taking a toll on me. I was like author Cornelius Ryan dealing with my own longest day…of not masturbating. (Way more difficult than storming a beach and killin' Nazis.)

By 10:30 p.m., I was a raging loon. Angry and pent up, I was slightly more tense than little Regan in *The Exorcist.*

"From this creature of Porn, be gone, silicone! In the name of the VCR, the VHS tape, and the Holy Lotion.

The power of Jenna Jameson videos compels you.

The power of Jenna Jameson videos compels you."

(I also liked Chasey Lain.)

Only one rational thought was in my brain: one of the guys on staff had a tape that I hadn't seen. I'll just watch a little, see that I'm not missing out on anything, and then I'll be fine. Still in a good position. Not gonna lose this bet. (Not even twelve hours in, and I was slightly more delirious than the zombies in *28 Days Later,* but hey, this was a good plan for now, and it made even more sense at the time.)

I bullet-trained over to North Hill and found the staff member in question. After a demanding, begging, drug-addicted plea, I wrangled away the sacred videocassette. ("Where is the Precious?") I came across as slightly less pathetic than the crack addict with the hamburgers from *Menace to Society.* But hey, it was worth it because now I had this shining beacon of VHS glory in my hands.

Back to the staff lounge. Nobody awake and I'll just watch a little bit of what have we here *Shane's World.* Well, this is some classy stuff. This girl, Shane, and her hot friends travel around the United States and have sex. Let the naked lady boobie brigade begin. Excuse me, I mean the classy naked lady boobie brigade.

At 7:00 a.m. the following day, there was an announcement on the PA system.

> "All senior staff are needed down at the parade ground."
>
> "Huh, what, where am I?"

I had passed out in the staff lounge. This was a first. I slept on a couch that was slightly less diseased than the Ebola virus containment center in Zaire. Up and out the door, no time to shave or brush my teeth. Shockingly this wasn't a concern to me. In fact, for some reason, I was in a pretty good mood. Now to make my announcement. But let's see what the rest of the senior staff were up to this fine and glorious morning. A magic cartoon bluebird literally descended from the treetops and perched on my shoulder for the walk from the staff lounge to the parade ground. We sang about sugarplums and dandelions.

> "Zip-a-Dee-Doo Dah, Zip-a-Dee-a. My, oh my, what a wonderful day."

No fucking way.

There everybody else was. I was running a little late, but that was OK because life was beautiful. They were all sitting there...raising a flagpole.

I walked up to the center of the staff. Then I slapped my hand down just like I was Kramer and pronounced, "I'm out."

Since I actually looked like Kramer back then, it wasn't a tough sell. In fact, I would like to think that with my spindly body and crazy hair, I played the part to perfection. See for yourself.

"You're out?" one of the directors asked.

"It hasn't even been twenty-four hours.."

"This was your stupid idea, and you're the first one out."

"Yes, gentlemen. I was seduced by Shane and her girlfriends, who took me through an exotic tour of locales throughout southern California and

> possibly the Arizona desert landscape. The scenery is stunning."

Domino one, the most rickety and masturbation-needy domino, had fallen. I was out faster than a number-sixteen seed in the NCAA tournament. Cue the press conference:

"We're just happy to be here. We just want to take it one play at a time and see what happens. Sure Kentucky is a good team, but we think we've got a pretty special program here at Prairie View A & M."

As the days wore on, the rest of the dominoes fell. One by one, they were all gone until only two were left standing: Clint and Allen. These guys had been the best of friends since 1994. To quote Jim Carrey in the underrated *Cable Guy*:

"Best friends. Forced to fight as enemies. Like Kirk and Spock on *Star Trek*. Da dadadada! Da dadadada!"

Days went by. Weeks went by.

The rest of us were good. We were back to our normal lives. Not these two guys. It was a war of attrition. I went up to Clint.

> "Who needs that nutmeg now, brother?"

Nothing like using a Malcolm X quote to needle the guy.

Meanwhile, Allen was good. He was holding fast. It was Secretariat versus Man o'War. The most exciting month-and-a-half in racing.

Oh, how things changed as time progressed.

Allen stayed eerily quiet. And content. Don't know why.

Not Clint. That guy was walking around with a gaunt, hollow look on his face. POWs at Cabanatuan had more fight in them than this guy did. He was beat down. I looked into his eyes.

"Clint, you OK? You good, buddy?"

My God. The man had no soul. Just an empty stare into the horizon. Before our very eyes he was becoming a Kardashian.

One month later, Clint caved.

Allen won because he had a secret weapon. His girlfriend visited him a couple times. Clint was alone and desperate. It was only a matter of time. Meanwhile I was the happiest number-sixteen seed of all time. Cue the presser.

> "We never wanted to be here in the first place. We had no business being in this game. Losing was awesome, and we're so glad it's over. Hopefully next year we can lose again, or better yet, we don't even get invited back to the tournament."

VII

Girls' Chapter

Top Five TV Show Episodes that Poke Fun at Scouting, Along with an Appropriate Quote:

1.) *King of the Hill*
"Order of the Straight Arrow"
"Wematanye calls them silence sticks to test your spirit of shutting up."
2.) *The Simpsons*
"Boy Scoutz 'n the Hood"
"Campers pampers."
3.) *The Simpsons*
"The Bart of War"
"Apu Nahasapeemapetalong: Preteen braves? Is this another one of those community youth groups that inhabit the culture of those you invaded and destroyed?"
Marge Simpson: "Exactly the preteen braves."

4.) *South Park*
"Cripple Fight"
"Cripple Fight!"
5.) *The Flintstones*
"Cave Scout Jamboree"
"Old MacDonald" sung by children from around the world.

We were sitting around one day, talking. Nothing in particular, just talking.

Then one of the staffers, Mike Barilla, hits us with it:

"Guys, I've got a question."

"Yeah, Mike."

"I don't know if I'm a virgin or not."

"Well, Mike. It's pretty straightforward. You either are or you aren't. What seems to be the confusion here?"

Mike began. . . "I met this girl, and she was, like, thirty, and she was pretty hot, and she flew me out to New York."

Disclaimer: Mike was about eighteen when we had this conversation. The gods blessed him with ridiculous good looks. Any story about him being flown to New York was plausible because he was the George Clooney of Catalina. He was my only friend who made my wife stutter and stumble when she met him. We bumped into him a couple years later while he was chopping meat in the grocery store. There he was, looking all seductive, *Two Moon Junction*-style, and my wife tripped over her words when she met him.

Back to the story at hand.

Mike continued. "So she flew me to New York, and then we did it…in the butt. That was it, though. We only had butt sex. So am I a virgin?"

I have never gotten a straight answer to this question. If I travel to Paris right now, sneak into the Louvre, meet up with Opus Dei, draw the appropriate pentacle on the chest to summon the Vitruvian Man, and unlock the coded spherical cylinder, it will literally read verbatim,

"WE, THE INNER SANCTUM, HAVE NO IDEA IF MARK DOTH BE A VIRGIN FROM THINE HAVING BUTT SEX. THOU HAST STUMPED THY PRIORY OF SION."

—∞—

For some people, getting girls at camp was a rite of passage. For other people (read: me), it was the thrill of the chase…right up until the part where the car crashes in spectacular, flaming fashion. For our group of guys on staff, it was a free-for-all pursuit if and when you thought you had a lead on some tail.

Back in 1992, my first summer on staff, I remember the first conversation I ever had with somebody about meeting girls.

"Seth, man, I met this chick today."

"Oh, that's cool, Marvin."

Marvin was my cabinmate and, again, a really good-looking guy. Also he was smarter than me and more popular, so I pretty much hated him and prayed daily that he would get hit by a canoe paddle and lose his looks and his cranial capacity. Nice guy, though.

Marvin continued.

> "Yeah, she's a total Betty [horrendous word right there, but factually accurate circa 1992]. Anyway I'm supposed to meet her later on tonight. I need her to think that I'm in college. She's like a Mormon chick, and I think she goes to UC–San Diego or something. What do you suggest?"

An idea popped into my head. It was becoming clear…there was a kid in my class today wearing a hat, and if I could just make out the letters on the hat, then I would have my answer, and Marvin would have his fake university degree. The letters were B…Y…U…

I was a fucking genius!

"Dude, Marvin, tell her you go to BYU."

"Seth, I'm pretty sure that's a Mormon school."

"No it's not, dude. This kid in my nature class was wearing a BYU hat."

Marvin continued. Surprisingly he wasn't sold on my argument.

"I think so, dude. It's a Mormon school or at least some Mormons go there."

"No way, Marvin. It's not a Mormon school. It's in Utah" (the defense rests).

I think between 4:00 p.m. and our free time after dinner, Marvin transferred from BYU and earned his faux-baccalaureate elsewhere before he met up for his sweet lady lovin'.

Other people at camp were having sex. They were meeting yachtees' daughters or importing their girlfriends. Some guy at camp even got a hand job on the beach. I was some guy at camp. I was on the beach. Where was my hand job? Ask not what your hand can do for you, but what you can get some girl's hand to do to you instead.

This was awful. Plus I went zero sperm body count my first summer at camp. I didn't even touch myself for fear of being busted on *To Catch a Masturbator*. (More on that fun story later.)

Evan Foglehorn was a guy I worked with for a few summers. He not only had sex on staff, but he got caught. And it was fuckin' awesome. Foglehorn was in his cabin, having actual sex with his actual girlfriend, and his cabinmate walked in. Foglehorn took one look at his roomie and immediately started yelling, "Come on, buddy! Let's go! Eiffel Tower, man. *EIFFEL TOWER*!"

For those of you who are not in the know, this is what the Eiffel Tower looks like:

In 1999, again, my last summer on staff, I threw everything—including the kitchen sink—at trying to get laid.

Dancing at the Isthmus with a girl and even making out with her, I was actually making progress. My tongue was tasting sweet, sweet tonsil action. My good friend Allen pulled me aside to deliver the bad news. She was seventeen. The band Winger made that seem so cool. It wasn't. I proceeded to keep trying to make out with her, but hey, at least I stopped giving her alcohol once I found out how old she was.

It's called integrity, people!

The next week, I met an eighteen-year-old girl, and again, my friends told me she was too young. Then five minutes later, she was with Foglehorn. The man was a monument to smooth and sophisticated. What kind of monument you ask? An Eiffel Tower, baby!

The summer was drawing to a close, and it looked like all hope was lost.

"But there was another."

Kailey.

Kailey was an EMT and our camp doctor for the week. But she was more than that. She was a heavenly angel descended from the majestic desert landscape of Norwalk, California. More specifically, she was a hot blonde at camp, and I really wanted to have sex with her...solely out of love. All I needed with Kailey was an opening. (Don't be crass.) I needed an isolation play. Carmelo has the ball in the post, and he's calling a clear-out to win the game. I needed my own clear-out isolation play. But how?

My fucking friends were always around me. Stupid friends. I needed something. Then one night, I caught a break. As I was walking back to my A-Frame rehearsing a conversation I would have with my future summer-camp girlfriend and life-love, I was approached by a scoutmaster and a scout.

"Excuse me, sir. Are you on staff?"

"Yes, I am. How can I help you guys?"

"Well, Bobby here isn't feeling so good. Do you know where the camp doctor might be?"

This is so fucking awesome. I needed an excuse to see Kailey, and I've got a dying kid on my hands. Thank you, Jesus.

"Oh no, are you OK, buddy? You a little sick?"
(Please be terminal, please be terminal.)

Scoutmaster: "He's got a fever, I think. I'm sure it's nothing."

"No, no. You know what? It's no trouble at all. Let's go up and get the camp EMT. You can't be too careful."

(Anything for the kids—and Kailey's awesome hotness.)

After taking Tiny Tim and his scoutmaster to Kailey's cabin, I knocked ever so gently.

"Uh, heh, Kailey. It's Seth. You know, the (*awesome*) Nature Director (*who worships you and is technically*

> *stalking you*). I hate to trouble you, but I'm with a scoutmaster here, and one of his scouts, little Timmy (Bobby—whatever!), is kind of sick. They asked for the camp doctor (*And I know where you live because I'm your "Single White Female.*).

Kailey came out of her cabin. She looked the dying patient over and, miracle of miracles, she brought him back from the dead. (Advil.)

Now Kailey and I were off to the dining hall for some sweet, sweet…wait for it…hot cocoa.

We had a nice conversation for a few minutes.

> "Sorry I had to bug you, Kailey. I just wanted to make sure he was OK. Seemed like a good kid." (Damn, I'm smooth and sophisticated. Gentlemen: Prepare for Eiffel Tower launch.)

Even with no one around, I was tragically aware of where my efforts were going. Kailey firmly placed me in the fast lane of her friendship track.

All I could think about was the poor scout who was feeling sick and how he was on death's front door—and how mad I was at him now.

I PRETENDED TO BE INTERESTED IN YOU, SICK KID. ALL YOU NEEDED WAS SOME GODDAMN ASPIRIN! DAMN YOU, JOEY (BOBBY—WHATEVER)!

My vow of unintentional abstinence carried on for the rest of that summer. It wasn't until the following year that I brought out my then-girlfriend to camp to visit, and then *finally* my dry spell was broken. Ironically as happy as I was to finally get some camp lovin', I was still too lazy to go to the isolated backwoods of camp. Instead I opted for the "totally romantic" and "discreet" tent city within walking distance of literally everybody. As we started to get down, one of the guys on staff walked right by our tent, while having a nice conversation with his father since it was also parents' weekend. The long-and-dry season was over, and there were two witnesses (proof!)—and then I didn't get any more the rest of the weekend that my ex-girlfriend visited me.

VIII

Attack of the PC Movement

Top Five Most Obscure Merit Badges Ever Offered by the Boy Scouts (Wikipedia):

1.) Pigeon Raising
2.) Stalking
3.) Hog Production
4.) Master-at-Arms
5.) Rabbit Raising*

*As I recall, there were three requirements to earn this merit badge:

1. Buy rabbit
2. Raise rabbit
3. Sell Thumper to slaughterhouse ("Bunny's Gone")

In 1994, my third summer working at Catalina, we had a new Director introduced to Camp. He was from a new school of thought that stressed feelings and emotions, and being kind to people. He endorsed the philosophy of being Politically Correct. According to Wikipedia, "Political Correctness is a term which denotes ideas, policies, and behavior" and blah blah blah blah blah. I don't know what all those fancy words and phrases mean, but it was sheer torture for a nineteen-year-old kid. It started innocently enough when PC3PO told us, "Let's all put on our rose-colored glasses" in dealing with the scouts. I'm too stupid to know what that actually means, but somehow, I think it meant we couldn't make fun of the little bastards. That was step one. But Metta World PC was just gettin' started. Then we realized he had a plan for our Saturdays.

Saturday was the last day of camp. To clarify, this was when one group of the little bastards (read: scouts) mentioned above vacated the premises, and we had a full twenty-four hours of calm before the next storm of whiny, needy, merit-badge grubbers arrived. Our attire and demeanor that day was as passionate and professional as the Iraqi soldiers assigned to defend Saddam's Palace during the "mother of all battles" against the infidel American invaders during Desert Storm. With the difference being that at least those guys were in uniform and cared about their appearance. Also, their boss didn't make them wear stupid pirate hats. We gave those kids a meal of sloppy Joes and shoved them onto a boat and told them goodbye. Our care-o-meter was wilted down to zero, and only twenty-four hours of excessive alcohol imbibing could fill our hearts with love again.

The PC Maker (George Clooney and Nicole Kidman-movie about a terrorist armed with mobile nukes…never mind) told us we needed new uniforms for departure Saturday. I had a Saturday uniform. Those kids got to see me in ratty scout shorts, busted Teva flip-flops, and a surly attitude to boot. What more could I possibly need? Well, now I had a new uniform as well to go along with my "leave-me-alone" personality: we were Saturday morning pirates. The PC Fashion Police expected we would dress like pirates to "Give the wee sea dogs a landlubber's parley as they walked the plank above Davy Jones's Locker."

Fuck me!

As a pirate, I would now have to wear an eye patch, a big, goofy pirate hat, striped pants, vest, gold coins, and, of course, a big poofy white shirt, just like from that one episode of *Seinfeld*. (Thatone episode of *Seinfeld* we never wanted to re-create.)

I asked my superiors, "Do I have to wear all this stupid gear on Saturday morning?"

> "Yes you do, Seth. It's for the kids so they have a lasting memory to take with them on their boat ride home."
>
> "But they've been here all week. Haven't we given them a lifetime of lasting memories?"
>
> "No, Seth, we haven't. Every moment is precious in the development of their young adolescent minds, especially the pirate Saturday ensemble we wear for the kids as they leave on the boat home. You should be proud to be a pirate for these young scouts."

There was no way I was going to win this AAARRRgument.

I felt like Jennifer Aniston in *Office Space*.

"Now, Seth, fifteen is the minimum amount of doubloons you need in your scalawag's booty. You don't want to be known as a pirate who plunders the bare minimum, do you?"

Years earlier, I scoffed at going out with a girl who worked at Hot Dog on a Stick because of her atrocious uniform (because I could afford to be so picky). Now I was a fruity pirate with a fake plastic sword starring in *Pirates of the Native American Archipelago: Curse of the African-American Pearl.*

It got worse.

Later on in the summer, I was pulled aside by the Old Man and the PC for a very serious talk.

"Seth, I notice that you say things that are very sarcastic. And it causes a negative vortex of disingenuity."

(Huh? What?)

"Anyway, Seth, I think you should try to give up sarcasm for the rest of the summer and see what happens, see how good you feel."

"Uhm, OK. I can try, I guess."

What the hell. I can be a team player…or a total pussy.

The next twenty-four hours were tortuous.

Scouts and staff asked me questions (stupid questions), and I had to answer respectfully.

Cue the naïve, young Boy Scout:

> "Excuse me, Mr. Staff Person, I'm looking for the waterfront for my canoeing class. Where do I go?"

(It's five miles back in camp.)

(There's no waterfront at Emerald Bay on Catalina Island.)

(It's past the haunted murder ghost parade ground and at the Great White Shark Feeding Center.)

> "Oh, hey. Such a great question, little buddy. Just keep walking down past the dining hall, and you can't miss it. You're a great scout."

Then it was the camp director asking, "Seth, can you help unload the supply boat? We need a few extra hands."

(No! I'm busy.)

(If I help unload the supply boat, how many boxes of candy do I get for being such an amazing human being?)

(Don't we have kitchen staff who should be doing this?)

> "Oh, sure. I would be glad to help. Anything that's good for the camp is great for me. Just want to be a team player."

After two full days of playing a Stepford Wife, I couldn't take it anymore. Why would I have ever agreed to work at a

Boy Scout Camp if I couldn't make fun of the scouts. So I crawled back into my old skin, replete with sarcasm and surly demeanor. Aaaahhh, it's good to be home.

But it got worse. I was twenty-thousand leagues under the PC. Big Brother walked into my cabin for a surprise inspection. Then he reprimanded me for looking at pornography. "You know, Seth, pornography isn't part of the scouting way. I don't think this is what Lord Baden-Powell had in mind when he invented the Boy Scouts."

Oh, I'm sorry. I forgot that when Lord Baden-Powell was foraging through South Africa during the Boer Wars, he didn't have time to look at some big ol' *National Geographic*-style titties. My mistake. I was looking at my buddy's *Easy Rider* magazine that had one airbrushed chick on page seven. It wasn't even mine, and for God's sake, it was certainly not pornography. I know pornography. "Me and porn we were like peas and carrots."

And in this magazine, Alexia kept her clothes on... "mostly.. . mostly."

The last straw was broken at the lip-sync competition. At Emerald Bay, two things mattered. Well, technically three things mattered, but since I couldn't get a girl, two things mattered. They were the lip-sync competition and the annual Broomball tournament. (More on broomball later.) The lip sync was a rite of passage. New staff members did some terrible song cover, got booed mercilessly by the senior staff, and then went back to the drawing board for a year. Well, my days of being chased off the stage were over. I had been planning for more than a year what to do with our song.

Clint, Jake, and I worked together throughout the day in preparation for the lip sync. Jake was a happy-go-lucky kid from Flagstaff, Arizona, who was always down to hang out and be a part of the team. He also had a mean streak in him that only came out in competitions. He wanted to win as bad as Clint and I did. On a sad note, many years later, Jake was struck down with a terrible, pathetic addiction that absolutely crippled him called fantasy baseball.

This lip sync was our time to shine. We spliced together a mix of George Clinton's "Atomic Dog" with *The A-Team*, classical music, and some funny lines from *Coming to America* all interwoven into a phantasmagoric supercalifragilistic voyage of awesomeness.

The lip-sync competition was always fierce. Nilius and his buddies one year did a tag-team lip-sync dance-off to the Spice Girls' "Wannabe."

Comedy was watching muscled-up Nilius get a regulation Boy Scout belt placed on his chest as a Posh Spice-style bra and screaming, "I don't care if it hurts me! You make sure that it holds me up! We need to win, damn it!"

Meanwhile, two guys on staff, Kerry and Stephen, just performed to "I'm Too Sexy" by Right Said Fred. They were vicious.

Now it was our turn. And we were awesome. I ran the microphone like I was Axl Rose at the Whiskey. I owned my audience. Clint and Jake staged a transcendent ballet that was equal parts *Black Swan,* equal parts John Wu gunfight. At the very end the song stopped, and then Clint and I came together to recite the following lines from the movie *Coming to America* from the scene where the old guys from the barbershop talk amongst themselves after going to see Randy Watson at the community center. These lines were added to our mix.

"God damn, he good."

"God damn, that boy can play."

It was time for the judges to tally final scores. Judge number one: good; judge number two: solid; and judge number three: excellent. We took third place. I had always been dead last in this event, like a fat Kelly Clarkson. (Oh, wait, she won.)

Well, now we were in third place. We had a Bronze Medal.

AND THEN IT HAPPENED.

The Thought Police chimed in:

> "You know, I noticed that at the end of Seth's song, they took the Lord's name in vain. I'm pretty sure that's not in the *Scout Handbook*. In fact, I think that violates the Twelfth Commandment of Scouting: being reverent. I think the judges need to deduct some points from his team's overall score."

Oh my God. There was no way this was happening. Two years ago, a guy performed "Wasting Away Again in Margaritaville" while holding up a small army of his own personal liquor bottles, for Christ's sake (oops, not being reverent there). He did this with an assortment of scouts and scoutmasters watching from just outside the dining hall.

Now I was being penalized. This was absolutely unprecedented.

> "Congratulations, George Mason, on your historic run to the Final Four. You did something virtually unheard of for a midmajor conference school, and what's that, hold on a second? One of your players sent an impermissible text message to his dying grandmother who has leukemia while your AAU coach was visiting her at St Jude's, and you did this during the no-contact period? We're going to need your Final Four banner returned immediately."

Utterly ridiculous. And there was nothing I could do except sit and enjoy my fourth-place finish. ("And there was much rejoicing…yaaay.")

Fortunately this was the only summer where the GOPC served in a leadership role with me. After 1994, he served in an auxiliary position and would visit from time to time, but he never had the same control over our thoughts and actions that he did that one summer. I would eventually get my day in the spotlight at the lip-sync competition, but not that year. Not until he was a nonfactor in my life at Catalina.

IX

The 'Mess' Hall

The 5 best ways to say grace before mealtime at Boy Scout Camp

1.) Have a kid from your troop go up there, yell "GRACE" as loud as possible, and then everybody runs into the dining hall as fast as possible can so you guys can eat first.
2.) "Yeah God, Boo Devil" (Simple, timeless classic)
3.) "Johnny Appleseed"
4.) Grace in Hebrew. Truth be told, I'm not particularly religious but I always liked watching the other kids in camp get uncomfortable because they didn't know what was being said up there, especially if the kid chanting went on a little too long and made the Christian and Mormon kids wait even longer before they could get their tater tots.
5.) The Ricky Bobby Grace "Dear Lord baby Jesus, lyin' there in your ghost manger, just lookin' at your Baby

> Einstein developmental videos, learnin' 'bout shapes and colors. I would like to thank you for bringin' me and my mama together, and also that my kids no longer sound like retarded gang-bangers.

The dining hall at camp was where we congregated three times a day. This was both as a scout as well as when I worked on staff. The dining area at a summer camp was a circus tent. There was theatre, songs, jokes and I was always entertained. My first year at camp as an actual camper was in 1986 and one day I made the mistake of not agreeing with one of the older kids in our troop, a 15 year old who suffered from PTSD after watching the movie Platoon. Our generalissimo thought that scouting was the army, and I was one of his cadets that needed to be whipped into shape. My transgression, as I recall, was having a birthday the week we were all at Emerald Bay. Our Field Marshall in training decided that to celebrate me turning 12, he would feed me a meal down my pants.

I know right now you're asking yourselves, how is it possible to eat a meal down your pants. Well, let me tell you, it's not as challenging as you might think. The first thing this kid did was, he took a glass of camp punch and pulled back my scout shirt. Then he poured the glass down so that I wouldn't be thirsty. It's important you don't get dehydrated when you're outside all day. No big deal right, it's not like your clothing gets stained, especially not from cherry kool-aid. Then, he sent some salad down with the juice. Truly it would be a crime if I ate no vegetables, so I guess he kind of had my best interests at heart. Then came the tacos and

Mexican rice, as well as some chocolate cake for desert. After this meal was over I decided that for the first time that week, I probably needed to take a shower.

The great part of this diet was that there was no way I would put on weight, which is important when you're in a Boy Scout troop in the celebrity-obsessed culture of Southern California. Someday I truly hope that if this book inspires a new diet craze, 'the meal down the pants diet', that I get my due credit for being the first to try getting camp jungle juice poured down my back. I don't think anybody even got in trouble for this little stunt. Really, this was just a bunch of kids keeping themselves entertained at mealtime.

As we got older we discovered that tricks which worked on us when we were younger scouts were now perfectly available to be used on the new scouts on our troop.

I would start off the conversation, and generally one of the other senior kids in my troop, like my friend Alvin would chime in to lend added credibility.

"Hey guys, before we eat breakfast, who brought the bacon stretcher?"

I would turn to Alvin.

"Oh yeah, that's right." Alvin responded. "If we don't have a bacon stretcher then we get 30% less bacon. It's too bad I left mine in camp next to the left-handed smoke shifter."

(They're both made by the same company.)

We would turn to the new scout. Let's call him Timmy.

"Hey Timmy, can you do us a favor? Can you see if one of these troops has a bacon stretcher? We really need one before breakfast."

Now once the kid took off he usually came back five minutes later. This was because some scoutmaster pulled the kid aside and told him that there was no such thing as a bacon stretcher, except in Wisconsin.

Once we tried this at a Boy Scout Camporee, and instead of having the kid go around the dining hall, we told him to go to the campsite about 200 yards away, because our campfire was going to make our eyes water, unless of course we had the coveted left handed smoke shifter. After he left we went back to our normal daily events. 45 minutes later this kid came back and ran right up to me. He did not look happy.

"You guys suck alright. I went to the next campsite over and they told me they lent their smoke shifter to another troop. Then I went to the next campsite and those guys said the same thing. I went to four campsites before I realized you guys were playing a joke on me."

There was a full-on half a second pause before we all broke down laughing. This kid was a good sport because he started laughing too. I even apologized and told him that by the time he was a senior scout in our troop he could summon the younger kids to get the solar powered soap dispenser or the underwater basket weaving kit. Seriously though, what were the odds though that every other troop would be in on the joke. That was priceless.

Years later, when I was back with my troop at another Scout Camp called Whitsett, we had another meal monstrosity that became the subject of lore in our troop. For whatever reason, the meal wasn't great that night. One of the kids in our troop, Owen, was bored and started mushing his meal together. He used his fork to mix his roast beef, mashed potatoes, green beans and desert together into a big swirling pile. The scoutmasters weren't thrilled that he was wasting food, and that's when one of our kids came up with what I regard as a great idea;

"Hey Owen, how much money do you want to eat what's on your plate."

Owen looked up from his food. Now he wasn't just some bored scout staring into his abyss of mashed-up dinner. He was a competitor.

"It's gotta' be big money dude. I'm not going to eat this for nothing."

"Well what about a dollar."

(The high rollers were at the table.)

"Let me see the dollar."

"Well I don't have one but maybe. . . "

At this point, every kid in the troop reached into their pockets. Trading-post candy be damned, we had to sacrifice our quarters so we could watch Owen throw a blended camp roast beef smoothie down his gullet.

Like a country scrambling to avoid defaulting on their creditors, we came up with our dollar at the last possible minute.

Owen grabbed the fork and loaded up his first bite of food.

Suddenly, his older brother Brendan got up. Damn't, I thought to myself. We were going to have some fun at Owen's expense, and now Brendan was going to make his kid brother stop because he was trying to protect him. That's not fair. (Truth be told, I was probably jealous that I didn't have an older brother to protect me.)

Brendan addressed the table;

"Hey guys, here's another dollar. Owen, you get this if you kill the pitcher of punch."

(Clearly I misread the older brother-younger brother relationship dynamic)

Two whole dollars. Holy shit, that was some crazy camp money. Imagine walking into the Trading Post with that crazy bitcoin. Mambas and Now-A-Laters were 40 cents a pack and that $2.00 could buy almost. .. well, you get the idea.

Owen started eating. He shoveled in that food bite after bite like he was John Candy in *The Great Outdoors* eating 'The Ol' 96er.' In between, he was going Three 6 Mafia with it and "sipping on some Camp Punch." After a few minutes the food was gone. Then, like the drunk at the bar who didn't want to get cut-off, Owen kept on pouring himself cups of punch. And yes, in case you were wondering, it was cherry kool-aid. Owen went through another three glasses. I shared a tent with Owen, and we were buddies, so it was important that I offered him moral support through this challenge.

"Hey dude, do you want to save some of my leftovers for breakfast? You could mix in everything with your milk and cereal. That would be good."

Other kids offered their support as well.

"Hey Owen, do you want some of the butter? Butter goes great after any meal."

Owen continued, undeterred by our probing statements.

Finally, he had one last glass of punch left. That was all that stood between him and enough money to corner the

Trading Post market. Owen started to sip. We all counted down in unison;

"Five."

Owen drank.

"Four"

Owen kept drinking

"Three"

Owen was drinking, but a little slower now.

"Two"

Owen stopped drinking. . . and he put his hand on his stomach.

Suddenly, his glass started to fill-up. That was weird I thought. Normally people drink juice. They don't pour juice out of their mouth into a cup. Then it hit me. Owen was about to blow chunks. All of a sudden the cup filled-up to the brim. Then the cup runneth over. Now Owen was vomiting in pink Hello Kitty colors all over his plate, the table and our bench seating. He tried to run away, but literally he kept vomiting out everything in his system. The guy probably needed water, but we were all laughing too hard to help him. Finally, after what seemed like an eternity, Owen stopped throwing-up. Every other troop in the dining hall was watching Owen's performance in awe, no doubt jealous that they didn't come up with our idea first.

The comments came in immediately.

"Dude, that was amazing. You were like that guy in Stand By Me. Now we all need to barf."

"Can you do it again Owen? Please, Please!"

Our scoutmasters left the table, presumably out of disgust, as well as to call a Hazmat team over with some towels. After they left, Owen's brother brought-up a very astute point.

"Owen, you didn't finish everything. I don't think you won the bet."

Two high profiled legal teams were hastily assembled to address Owen's competitive eating controversy. The Owen defenders responded by pointing out that he did in fact eat all his food. Then his detractors responded by saying that technically, Owen didn't finish his punch. Furthermore, the point of the bet was that Owen had to both consume his food as well as to keep it in his system for a little while. At this point, Owen was just sitting there, staring at the floor, and really he seemed kind of out of it. (Too bad none of his friends got him a glass of water. Man, we sucked.)

After much debate, a great compromise was reached. Owen would be given $1.00 for eating all the food on his plate, but the other $1.00 would not be his because technically, he still had some punch in his cup before he proceeded to yak all over camp.

(The system works!)

Lastly, it was very important that we moved on from this embarrassing event. The last thing we wanted to do was permanently scar Owen psychologically. He was our good buddy. Best if we just move on and pretend this never happened. We decided on the nickname 'Puker.'

Mealtime was even more fun when I was on staff. As a disclaimer, mealtime was great, especially if we didn't have to sit with the troops. The goal was to sit at the Director's table or in the back of the dining hall with my friends. We even volunteered to serve meals so that as a reward for slopping Joes onto plates we could sit with our fellow brothers on staff.

Still, our Program and Camp Director would come around and tell us that we needed to sit with the troops.

"Seth, you need to sit with a table of scouts for at least two meals a day. You should really only be at the Director's table for one meal."

"Sure guys. I promise that I will sit with a troop. The problem is that I don't want to take away from the bonding time that these kids really need with their fellow troop members."

This line of BS never worked. I did however find it in me to sit with a troop if one of their kids ever brought contraband to camp, namely Strawberry Quick or birthday cake from the mainland.

The only time we ever actively tried to sit with the troops was when we had the troop of hot girls from Orange County. Then it was all about ensuring that our campers were having a wonderful experience and appreciated all of the core values of scouting, especially the brunettes.

Sitting at the hot girl table proved to be near-impossible. That was like trying to get into Skybar in Hollywood on a Friday night without a VIP pass, and I was never on the list. Hot girls aside, our staff would generally congregate in the back of the dining hall and make fun of each other.

One thing I noticed working on staff was that nobody had a problem eating food off of somebody else's plates. We were like a tribe of groomer monkeys in the wild being observed by that chick from the movie 'Aliens.' I would routinely watch our Program Director have a grown-up conversation with somebody across the table, while the people on his left and right side would reach over and grab his brownies, his rice krispy treats, even the sacred Tater Tots (hallowed be thy name.) Ironically, you needed a bad meal once in awhile just so that you didn't have to share. Or you could go to the salad bar, but that wasn't an option we ever considered. Salad took away valuable plate space, plate space best reserved for fried food, and that's what this country is all about. "Merica!"

One year, they decided to play music in the dining hall. This made sense. The kids got upbeat music and it seemed to make the dining hall a little more cheerful. Everybody from the staff to the scouts to the scoutmasters loved this arrangement. I mean who could possibly complain about a little Top 40 music or some classic rock at the dinner table? What we didn't reckon on was that there was a new type of person at camp, and that was 'The Attachment Mom.' Attachment parents, as far as I can tell, are moms who are emotionally closer to their kids and show them undue amounts of love so that those kids are more in touch with their feelings when they're getting bullied. One day, one of these moms, who was also a scoutmaster, decided to speak to the staff about their abhorrent choice of music.

She entered and sought out the dining hall manager.

"I noticed that you are playing inappropriate songs at mealtimes. I don't like the themes that are are being underscored in this music."

The dining hall manager responded;

"It's the Beatles."

"Yes, I know. And this song is inappropriate."

I personally didn't know any inappropriate Beatles songs. This particular song was called 'I Am The Walrus.' Maybe this was the one where you could play it backwards and hear them say "Paul is dead." All I knew was that if I was the dining hall manager, the kids would have been serenaded with 2 Live Crew lyrics breakfast lunch and dinner. Kids on my watch would get to eat their morning fruit loops while listening to Luther Campbell sing;

"Freaky Bitchez with plenty of Ass.

Rolling to the music and shaking real fast"

(Probably a good thing that I was never hired into the dining hall manager position.)

Attachment mom continued;

"My son is 15 and he's had some serious life events that he's had to deal with in his short time on earth. These lyrics contain mature themes. There is a line in here where the Beatles say "pornographic priestess" and that might encourage my son to lapse back into questionable behavior."

The dining hall manager apologized and told her that he would refrain from playing such harsh lyrics. At the next meal he didn't have another playlist cued up on his ipod and he didn't want Attachment Mom coming after him, so he chose not to play any music at all.

Attachment mom was not happy with this arrangement.

Again, she sought out the dining hall manager.

"I said no inappropriate music. That does not mean no music whatsoever."

Wow, I guess she channeled her inner Kevin Bacon and went all Footloose with it, demanding the right to listen to music. In your face town hall meeting!

For the next meal our dining hall manager figured better give her what she wants, but play it safe. He put classical music on the stereo.

Anyone want to guess who wasn't happy listening to Mozart over dinner?

Attachment mom let her opinions be known;

"You know, when I said play music, I didn't mean something so boring. I mean this isn't very upbeat at all. In fact, I don't think any of the kids here like classical music."

Probably true, but this certainly wasn't the week we got to blast some 2 Live Crew onto the speakers. Those guys were bonafide experts at dealing with mature themes. They rapped about some of the most important issues of their day, namely stripclub décor and etiquette.

"Girls in the back dancing in cages,

Guards out front armed with gages."

Although our time with Attachment Mom was limited, I will be forever grateful at her for warning me of the dangers of listening to the Beatles. If only she could have traveled back in time to warn Ed Sullivan as well.

Another great part about eating at camp was that no trick was too juvenile. You could unscrew the salt shaker or pour salt into the napkin dispenser and it never got old, especially when somebody got mad at you. After loading up the salt into the napkin dispenser and watching my bouncing betty landmine work to perfection, I received a very angry reaction from one of my fellow staffers.

"What if I pulled the napkin out too fast Seth? The salt could have blinded me and then how would you have felt?"

"I don't know, probably kind of hungry. Can you pass the ketchup?"

My freshman year at college, one of the seniors on the volleyball team taught me this trick that I couldn't wait to bring to camp. He grabbed a fork at lunch and proceeded to pretend to stick the fork in his eye very slowly. It was really uncomfortable to watch. Then, he said;

"This isn't working. Screw it!"

He took the fork in his left hand and rammed it through his right hand, which was cupped up, into the eye. All of a sudden all this white stuff squirted out of his hand. (I guess we were going to need a new Team Captain now.)

In the cupped hand he had hidden a coffee creamer. The fork hit the creamer, and viola,he made it look like eye goo squirting everywhere.

When I brought this trick to camp with me I was a bonafide rockstar. I was David Copperfield every single week since I could do this trick in front of a brand new audience. Each and every single day an army of kids aged anywhere from 10-15 years old went crazy at all my dining hall shenanigans. I was so in awe of my powers that I decided to take my show on the road.

My friend from staff, Jackson, invited me to hang out with him at the dorms at UCLA. My semester was over and

Jackson's was wrapping up in a couple weeks time, so I figured why not go over to UCLA. Word on the street was there might be some pretty girls there.

Jackson and I played some basketball, checked out his dorm and then he informed me it was time to go get lunch. He was on the meal plan so we would be eating in the dining hall on campus. We sat down and next thing I knew, three pretty girls sat down across from us. I looked around. There were no other guys in the room. It was me and Jackson and that was it. No fraternity brothers, no varsity athletes, no 'Reality Bites alt rock grunge rock stars which for some thing girls were kind of into back then. Nope, it was just us. I was hangin' with the ladies and there was no way whatsoever I could screw this up.

Then I decided to speak.

"Hey do you guys want to see my eye trick? It's really cool."

Before I got an actual answer, (with no being the actual answer), I grabbed a fork, jammed it into my eye and shot coffee creamer all over the table.

All three of the girls glared at me before they responded.

"It's finals week right now."

"We don't need this."

"Shouldn't you guys be leaving? You don't even go to this school."

The dining hall at boy scout camp was a magical place, a source of endless entertainment to all those involved, but those adventures didn't necessarily translate well into the real world.

X

Pranks

Five Celebrities Who Were Girl Scouts (momlogic.com):

1.) Lynda Carter (Wonder Woman!)
2.) Martha Stewart
3.) Mariah Carey
4.) Sheryl Crow
5.) Susan Lucci (It took her eighteen tries to get her Gold Award.)

Sven and I were running around frantically on the North Hill of camp. There were two hills that were bookends at the front of camp:They were North and South Hill. In between was the parade ground, where the scouts met for activities and assembled before mealtimes. Sven and I were on North Hill, and we had to dodge foot traffic or else we would be seen by the junior staff. We could neither be seen nor heard. Seal Team Six was on the prowl through the Hindu Kush of Catalina. More importantly, we were carrying a kayak.

> "What do you want to do with this thing, Seth?"
>
> "I don't know. Haven't really thought it through. Oh, I know. Let's put it in Tommy's cabin. Then we'll fill it with water. They're all asleep anyway."
>
> "But I thought Tommy was your friend."
>
> "And your point being..."

We crept up to the cabin. I opened the door with Sven picking up the rear and most of the weight of the watered-down kayak.

Tommy, half awake, half asleep, fully annoyed: "What are you doing?"

> "Dude. We're putting a kayak in your cabin."
>
> "No, you're not. Don't put a kayak in here."
>
> "Shut the fuck up, Tommy. You're going to wake everybody up and ruin my prank. We're putting this kayak here, got it?"
>
> "Fine. This is stupid."

Of course it was stupid. You didn't need an MD PhG from Harvird to figure out we were acting like morons.

After we placed the kayak down and filled it with water, I grabbed the shaving cream. Most people opt for the shaving-cream-in-the-hand prank, a timeless classic. For those of you who don't know about this, you place shaving cream in someone's hand and then use a piece of string or a feather (that's a little weird) to brush across their noses. The person then proceeds to move his or her hand over their nose. Works for me.

Hmm…who do we shaving cream?

Biscuit was asleep.

Who was Biscuit? Well, I'm glad you asked.

Biscuit was a FLK (funny looking kid) who only told stories that involved somebody he knew either dying or being in the process of dying. He was like an eighty-year-old woman who returns to Leningrad after the war, except this octogenarian was in the body of a fifteen-year-old boy.

A sample conversation:

> "Hey, Biscuit, what's going on?"
>
> "Hi, Seth. This kid in my troop, well, his dad's cousin was struck by lightning, and he's dead now. Also my friend from grammar school lost his uncle after he went bungee jumping at Half Dome. They're both dead. And, my science teacher's boyfriend was attacked by piranhas in South America last year. He's dead too. I just thought you'd like to know."
>
> "Wow, OK. Great talking to you, Biscuit."

Carvillak, howas no longer an angry, and yelling director, rather had become a calm and soothing leader with a sarcastic wit as well as my good friend. One day he just told this kid:

"I think I'm gonna call you Biscuit from now on."

The name stuck.

Biscuit was my canvas. While maneuvering around a submerged kayak, I proceeded to put some shaving cream on his face.

"Check it out, Tommy. He looks like a ghost."

"OK, it's funny, Seth. Now get out of here so I can go to bed."

—m—

Pranks were and still are an integral part of the camp experience. I didn't have fun at camp until I started pulling my first round of pranks. My gateway prank was taking a lobster skeleton and putting it into the toilet. Ten minutes later, one of the junior staff walked in, opened the lid, and I heard a "What the hell? Ha-ha."

Not my best work, but a good starting point. Sort of like a "My First Prank Kit by Hasbro."

Then Tommy and I were off. He was my "'Assistant to the Regional Manager' ," and I started referring to myself as the "After-Hours Camp Director."

For our first big-budget prank, we spent all of our lunch one day grabbing buzzbees (giant, slow, harmless horseflies that buzz very loudly) and putting them into trash bags. Then we walked into another cabin and released the buzzbees. ("Your firearms are useless against them! Save yourselves! Save yourselves!") The kids in that cabin came back from lunch and opened their door to a living botanical garden replete with fennel stocks, flowers, and a couple hundred buzzbees flying around. On the prank-o-meter scale, it was maybe a solid four out of ten.

Now it was time for our first crime-scene prank. This time, I couldn't find Tommy. Oh well, time to outsource. I grabbed a new staff member, and we went off to set up our first crime scene. It was year two, and this time, I had the good sense to bring some caution tape to camp with me.

New guy and I were walking around the campground after 10:00 p.m. (all is quiet). We were holding a rowboat, our roll of caution tape, and a plastic doll (all is well). The crime scene would be in front of the trading post. CSI Catalina would notice that the plastic Baby Jessica doll was found with an arrow in her back and a rowboat on top of her tiny little plastic head. (To quote Leslie Nielsen in *The Naked Gun*, "My uncle went the same way.")

We heard a noise…

Busted.

It was the camp director, Taylor, patrolling for wayward staff. We…looked…guilty.

What I wish I had said at that exact moment:

"Hey, Taylor, we were trying to give this chick an oar-gasm."

What I actually said:

"Uh, heh, Taylor, what's up? We're, uhm, uh, nothing. Uh, I'll go return this rowboat."

(I'm retarded.)

Taylor looked us over.

"Just make sure you put it back after breakfast tomorrow."

We had a green light. It was OK. Time to make our crime scene.

(Sometimes bosses could be cool. Unlike Mr. PC Frowny Pants, who would have told us that)

a.) An innocent female doll was being violated against her will by the white establishment;
b.) Rowboats were for rowing and rowing only; and
c.) I was exploiting child labor by using a member of the junior staff to assist with my prank.)

I had become a full-fledged prank monkey. If my buddy Carvillak gave me the green light, I was on it. This meant opening the flap to somebody's A-frame while they slept and lifting it as high as possible until it couldn't possibly go any higher. Then you let it fall with a thunderous crescendo so that the shockwaves reverberated through the A-frame, waking the sleeping victim. This prank was so much fun…until it was eventually done to me. Otherwise, it was so much fun.

If you stepped out of line or got lazy, you got the bucket of late-night water. Saltwater if you were on double-secret probation. If you gave alcohol to minors, it was a shaving-cream pillow pancake. I had become the Luca Brasi of pranks, and it felt good.

A few years later, we were going after a big fish. Darin Billison was our field sports director. Previously he had worked for the FBI. He worked on staff along with his two sons. One night, the nature staff met up for our fortnight of prankitude. All we wanted to do was place targets from the archery range in a circle around his A-frame. In the grand scheme of pranks, this really wasn't that exciting. If anything, it was us being too tired and lazy to do anything else.

We started to move archery targets around his A-frame. It was quiet. *Sooo* quiet. We had placed the first few targets and had completed almost a semi-circle.

Then we heard a faint noise, more like *ANGRYYELLING*!

> "I don't know who the hell you are out there, but I've got a gun, and if you so much as come after me and my kids, I swear to God I'll fucking shoot you where you stand."

Luca Brasi ran away like a scared little girl. We ran up north of camp, which was idiotic because now we had to work our way past his A-frame again to get back to our cabins. Somehow we slipped back into our cabins unharmed.

The next morning, I did what I had been doing since my freshman year of college. I slept in. This meant I missed morning colors.

When I got up and got moving, I was accosted by everybody on North Hill.

Jorge Dominguez was the best impressionist in camp, and he summed up the speech I missed that morning.

> "Dude, Jaffe. Darin Billison was pissed and he freaked the Hell out. It was awesome. He was cussing us out, and there was a scout troop there waiting

to present colors and they heard everything. It's all your fault, and you missed everything."

Herein is Darin Billison's speech, as it was dramatically reenacted by Jorge for me and the entire staff at least thirty more times that summer:

"Last night, somebody tried to attack our A-frame, and they vandalized camp property. Well, you jackasses don't know who you are fucking with because [wait for it] I AM A RETIRED FBI AGENT AND I SWEAR TO GOD YOU WILL NOT FUCK WITH ME AND MY FAMILY!"

That's right. He went Keanu Reeves with it. All he needed to do after that speech was grab his leg, fall to the ground, and shoot regulation scouting arrows straight into the air.

"AAAAAHHHHH!@!!!!!!!"

AHHHHGH!!

My last summer on staff, I just wanted one big prank to end with a bang. One that was effective, creative, and didn't involve somebody notifying Homeland Security about the code-red threat against his family.

Jonas was our camp orator. Every Friday night, he told a story to the scouts. The story he told that week was about the *Andrea Doria* and the *Stockholm*: two ships that collided at sea. After the campfire, we sat around and discussed Jonas's story.

I asked Clint and Alicia, one of the girls on staff, "What if it happened at sea?"

"It did happen at sea," Clint responded.

"What if it happened again, only this time on top of the dining hall?" I responded.

"What do you guys mean?" Alicia asked.

Alicia was a ridiculously hot girl from the strand in Newport Beach. A few years prior at camp (under the PC's watch, ironically), the staff had fully integrated with girls. This meant that a slew of hot girls from Orange County were running around camp and driving us crazy. We went from having one female cook with Eastern European grandma arms to becoming an open casting call for *The Hills*. Clint and I spent time with Alicia in the arcane and futile hope that one day, she might actually fall for one of us. And we liked her as a person. And we wanted to make out with her.

> "Well," I said, "what if we reenacted the collision of the *Stockholm* and the *Andrea Doria* on the roof of the dining hall?" (Nothing like a little international boat-crashing humor to lighten thecampers' spirits.)

So we were off.

There might have been eight to ten of us there. This went from prank to general spectacle. Fewer workers were hired to build the added lanes between the 405 and the 10 Freeway in west Los Angeles. We were like Christo with his giant umbrellas, and the roof of the dining hall was our posterboard.

We used a rowboat as the *Andrea Doria* colliding with a canoe marked *Stockholm*.

While thisprank was going on, a couple of staff guys decided to leave our prank and go after the waterfront director. This was ballsy. I mean this was another director, not just a regular member of staff. Everybody knows you don't go after a made guy, not unless you get permission from the heads of the five scout camps and only after you publicly say you got a beef with him. To further complicate matters, by which I mean make them more awesome, they were going after the first female director I had seen in almost ten years on staff. I don't know why her staff had had enough of her antics. Maybe it was because her ego trip of choice was to have her staff wash the rocks. Yes, you read me correctly. She would have a staff person wash down the rocks at the waterfront so that they didn't look so dirty. She would actually scream this command to whoever was in her crosshairs. Either way, the ignaceous hygiene monitor was fast asleep in her cabin. We didn't know this until Jake and I circled around camp and came back to admire our prank. We heard something. The bushes talked.

"What the fuck was that?"

"Is that you, Hargosy?"

"Dude."

Hargosy was an undergrad at USC who was majoring in weed, surfing, and possibly more weed. The guy made me sound like a poet laureate by comparison.

Hargosy continued:

"They're going after Calia."

"What do you mean?"

"Well, dude. They're going to lock her in her cabin and hit her with buckets of water."

(Shouldn't those buckets of water be used on the rocks instead?)

"I got the best seat, dude. You guys should watch."

Now, look. I know what you're thinking. Throwing ice water on a woman at night while she's asleep. Really?!But let me remind you that our government specifically does not classify waterboarding as torture, and furthermore, to not throw water at Calia because she was a girl, well, that would be downright sexist. The last thing any of us wanted was for Gloria Allred to go after the camp.

But forget about the moral ethical dilemma of giving a girl a wet T-shirt for a second. Don't you see what was happening? We were inspecting our prank while another prank was going on just one hundred yards away.

A prank within a prank.

We had reached our moment of Inception. Somewhere a top started to spin…

They approached Calia's cabin from the side and the front. At the front, she was barricaded in by a chair on the door. The barricaded chair door was an old Seth Jaffe favorite, but I was more than willing to let somebody else use one of my signature moves. Then the outer window slid open.

Whoosh!

Bucket number one went flying into her cabin.

Whoosh!

A second bucket. There was definitely a second bucket. The bucketeers ran.

Jake and I stayed with Hargosy to watch.

Now for the pièce de résistance.

We heard angry footsteps running for the door.

CRASH!!!

The door would not open.

Two more tries. Still no open door.

It was like watching the velociraptor trying to break out of its cage in the beginning of *Jurassic Park.*

The whole cabin looked like it was shaking.

RaAAAHHHH!!

Pause.

RAAAHHHH!

And then...it...the noise just...stopped.

The next morning, David Caruso from *CSI NY* walked up to the cabin and said:

"Well, gentlemen. It looks like the waterfront director met a tidal wave that washed her over."

Then we heard a riff from the Who: "YAAAY Dah dah dah!"

The last part of the first prank worth noting was that we took spare clothing from the honor box (read: lost and found) to make into people stranded at sea. OK, not so funny right at this moment, but back then, enough time had lapsed since the *Titanic* that we were good, and only our coastline was harmed during the Exxon Valdez oil spill.

For the finishing touch on our prank, we had stolen (liberated) custom-made life preservers from two different troops who both happened to be in camp that week. Both troops were from wealthy parts of southern California and stood out. You tend to be noticed when you have customized life preservers to go along with your speedboats. Ironically the two royal families of Catalina (our very own Kennedy's and Vanderbilt's) had an uneasy relationship. This probably stemmed from a conflict about not sharing inside information with each other when they pledged the Skulls. I wasn't certain.

In between the two boats, we had two fake people floating together in their rival life preservers, arm in arm. Expecting some blowback, we were pleasantly surprised when scoutmasters from both troops praised the innovation. That meant that we had brought peace and harmony to rival troops. Now they could form a life preserver-speedboat-trust-busting monopoly. It was my last prank ever working on the Island, and you can see the pictures for yourself.

IX

Homies and Dominoes

The Five Worst Movies Ever Made about Summer Camp:

1.) *Caesar and Otto's Summer Camp Massacre*
2.) *Meatballs II*
3.) *Meatballs III*
4.) *Meatballs IV*
5.) *A Summer Camp Nightmare*

My best friend at camp was a gangsta'. I mean, he actually was a gangsta'. His name was Davonte, and he was at the camp because he needed to straighten out his life. I was at camp to kill time between private school and college. We just had so much in common!

I wasn't from 'Tha' Hood' so naturally I had lots of questions for him.

"Hey, Davonte, what do those tattoos mean?"

"Oh, that's like if I stabbed somebody or if one of my homies was killed."

"Oh, that's nice."

"Hey, Davonte, what's it like in the hood?"

"I know this fool who got shot. But they got some fine-ass bitchez too."

Hmmm, fine bitches or get shot. Tough choice on that one.

"Hey, Davonte, will you teach me to play dominoes?"

"Maybe if you don't embarrass me like a little bitch."

Now we were talking. White Jewish kids in suburbia loved nothing more than hip-hop culture. That's why I had a Will Smith cassette tape. He was the happiest rapper I knew. Not only that, but my favorite episode *EVER* of *Beverly Hills 90210* was the one where the black family moved in next door, and I learned that, hey, that's OK. (I also was happy when Andrea started dating the Hispanic bartender.) Well forget that nonsense. Now I was going to learn me some dominoes.

Davonte outlined the rules.

> "You throw out a spinner. Then I play off it. Also, the numbers gotta match."
>
> "I'm listening."
>
> "And call out your fucking points. If you don't call 'em out, you don't get any of 'em."

OK, OK, got it. Tell the scoreboard operator I just scored a basket, otherwise we don't get our three-pointer. Sounds good.

> "Also, you're the bitch now, so you do the dishes."

If I was going to learn the game, I had to speak the speak. (Huh?)

> "OK, Davonte. I got the spinner thing down. What else?"
>
> "You don't grab bones until they're dealt. When you lose, you wash the bones."

I felt just like Lil' Chris in *Boyz in the Hood*.

> "Don't fucking go out of order either, dawg, I swear to God!"

"Got it."

"And if you go out on domino, you got to say it *LOUD*!"

"I will, dawg, cuz Ice Cube love dominoes but he don't want no drama ho's."

"Shut the fuck up, Seth."

"Yes, sir."

The other component to playing dominoes with Davonte and his homies was your drink. We used camp thermoses and the ratio had to be exact. It was very clever, by the way, because if you ever saw us stumbling around at midnight throwing up in the bushes, you knew we weren't drinking alcohol. We had camp thermoses with a Boy Scout logo on them, for God's sake. Boy Scout camp thermoses were specifically *not* made for consumption of alcohol. Ingenious!

Davonte's drink, as it would be listed on the recipe page of *Sunset* magazine:

¼ Lemonade

¾ vodkaAnd only a little ice, otherwise you were a bitch. (Again, just like in *Sunset* magazine.)

"Can I play my domino now?"

"No! You ask again in my hood, you get shot! But you lucky you my boy. I teach you!"

(If I got shot, did that mean I was also entitled to one fine-ass bitch to even things out? Maybe I'd ask later.)

Scoring was as follows:

Standard Points	**Street Points**
Five	Nick or Nick Nasty
Ten	Dime
Fifteen	Fidleen or Rape 'Em
Twenty	Dove Sac
Twenty-Five	Quarter
Thirty	Tres Dime (I may have invented this term as part of my initiation. Just like they do on Spike TV's *Gangland*.)
Thirty-Five	No term. Interesting note: This is the perfect game of dominoes, and I never actually saw anybody score a thirty-five. It's on my bucket list, provided that bucket is ¼ lemonade and ¾ Smirnoff. A'ight!

Davonte, his homie, Bravo, and I played dominoes from 9:00 p.m. until close to midnight every night. Occasionally somebody else would join into play for an hour or two. The fourth chair was a rotating guest chair like the one on *The Today Show*, assuming they played dominoes on *The Today Show* and told stories of homies who did time. Eventually I would fall asleep (read: pass the fuck out).

The next morning, I would wake up in a lemonade-vodka-infused daze.

> "Davonte, what happened last night? Hey, why'd you throw your shoe at me?"
>
> "Dawg, I tried to wake you up. I was having a threesome with the two girls from the kitchen."

There were, in fact girls on staff, as we already established. Girls being on staff had no bearing on my social life, but for other people it appeared to be a nice benefit. Davonte had magic ghettolicious charm that worked time and time again with the ladies. Getting them up to his vodka-lemonade-dominoes lair was his home-court advantage.

Since Davonte and his crew of misfits all worked in the kitchen, I never saw them during normal camp hours unless I had to serve meals or felt like checking in on my posse. If I ever actually said I was part of their crew, I think the ass-whipping would have been both severe and justified. I never knew what to expect when I visited the kitchen staff. When I walked through the kitchen I felt like one of those kids from the MTV special *Scared Straight*. I thought I was tough, but not until they laid it down for me.

One day when I walked in, Davonte and his boys—I mean boyz—were allat opposite corners of the kitchen holding small spatulas. There was cake mix in small lines on their arms and their aprons.

"Davonte, man, what's going on?"

Davonte explained:

> "Me and these fools, we play this game, right. We each take a cake spatula, and that's our weapon. Then, we put some frosting on our knives, and you gotta cut that fool on the other side of you before he stabs you back. Once you get stabbed, you dead."

Once you get stabbed, you dead. Wow! It was just like the show *Oz*, assuming that Adebisi shanked Poet with a shiv from Williams-Sonoma and that Poet bled Duncan Hines double moist chocolate cake-mix all over Emerald City.

My greatest memory of Davonte occurred during summer three at camp. I arrived late that summer. It was rare I could work the whole summer because of school, and besides, working half the summer was a good way to prevent burn-out. (That would be burnout, by the way, from working at a Boy Scout camp on a gorgeous island with no responsibilities in the world except drinking and trying to get laid.) On my first night in camp, I assessed my cabin. It was Davonte, two mean looking SOBs from the maintenance staff named Jorge and Manolo, and one prissy child of the private school system. If this was the movie *Alpha Dog,* I was the kid who wouldn't be around for the sequel.

At 11:00 p.m., the door opened. I was legitimately asleep, and my cabinmates barreled through. Davonte, Jorge, and Manolo jumped up in front of me, or "in my grill" as they might say, and started to talk:

> "Look. One of the rangers, you know, that white motherfucker, Edwin?"
>
> "Yes, I know that white motherfucker Edwin."
>
> "Well, he said some shit last week about a troop that was in camp from the hood. He was disrespecting these kids. They were sharp. They wore their uniforms, and they were good kids. Anyway he said something we didn't like, so we shaving creamed the fuck out of his stuff. If he comes by with the other rangers, we were here tonight and not a God damn thing happened."

Poor, poor Edwin. Unbeknownst to him, he brought a knife to a gunfight. One off-the-cuff comment, which he may or may not have made, landed him in Davonte's crosshairs. Once the shaving cream got involved, you better ramp up your border defenses.

You could do a lot of things at camp. Water ballooning and saltwater bucket bombs were par for the course in some circles. You could even throw somebody's clothing in the freezer. Shaving creaming somebody else's stuff, though, and not just their hand, well, that was different. Slowly I rolled out of bed.

> "OK, sure, Davonte. I'm tired. I'm sure nothing is going to…"

Knock, knock, knock.

I heard a pounding on the side of my cabin.

> "Seth. We want to talk to you."

It was Edwin and a posse of small rangers. He was as white as a ghost—a ghost who had just been hit with a roadside bomb made solely out of Barbasol. This was gonna be fun.

I opened the door partway to talk to them. Meanwhile, Davonte and the two extras from *8 Mile* waited on the blocked-off side of the door. Unless I could negotiate a peace settlement in the Middle East of camp, it was go time.

Edwin went first:

"I know Davonte is in there. I want him to come out. He shaving creamed all my stuff because of something he thinks I said."

> "Edwin, dude. Nothing happened. I swear we've been sitting here this whole time, chilling. Davonte really likes you. You guys are buddies. I don't know who shaving creamed your stuff, but it wasn't us. Besides I

just got here, and we were all just hanging out, talking about our girlfriends."

(If I was gonna' lie, I wanted a girlfriend for once.)

During a very long pause where Edwin circled around with a broken canoe paddle, my mind raced.

"OK, Seth. If I find out you're lying..."

"Not lying, dude. It's all good. Check on the other hill. It's probably some junior staff guy fucking around with everybody and not just you."

Slowly they left, and slowly I put my hand on the door handle. The second they were out of earshot, I closed the door completely. Davonte and the Thug Life Mafia jumped up at me and started laughing.

"Nice job, but you sounded nervous like a pussy. Good fucking job, though. Way to cover."

Jimmy Carter had just hammered out a successful peace accord between the Shaving Creamers and the Canoe Paddle Wielders, even though he sounded like a total fucking pussy.

XII

At the Isthmus Bar

The five most discussed movies amongst our staff while working at camp

1.) Independence Day
2.) The Blair Witch Project
3.) Blazing Saddles
*4.) Swingers**
5.) Point Break

Honorable mention: *Major Payne*

*I made the junior staff watch this movie one night, much to the chagrin of the camp director. For the rest of the summer, we had fifteen-year-old boys running around camp and telling each other, "You're like this bear man, with these fucking teeth…and she's this little bunny rabbit."

I was so desperate to meet girls one summer that I shaved my chest. In my heart of hearts, I knew this was the right move.

Removing my chest hair was the magic stepping stone to becoming a major-league player, the likes of which hadn't been seen at Catalina since the Cubs had spring training there in the 1920s.

It was very simple. One night, I went into the shower with a bottle of Nair. Me having a lot of hair, I knew I needed to use the entire bottle. Plus, I figured if I did this right once, I would never have to do this again for the rest of my life. Have a plan; work the plan.

I Nair-blasted my back, my arms, neck, and my belly in rapid fire. Then I waited. For a solid thirty seconds I felt nothing. Why do women complain so much about getting this done? This was easy. It was a walk in the OWO WOWOWWO OW OW OW! Oh my God, it was hurting so bad! I tried to splash cold water on myself, but it was getting stuck on my fingers, which were clogged full of Nair and hair. I flung water up, and 90 percent of it went through the hair interlaced between my fingers. The other 10 percent went up only an inch or so and then fell back directly onto my hands. It was so damn painful! While I was writhing in pain, I looked in the mirror. It was done. I was solidly removed of hair…with one possible exception.

I thought if I had chest hair and a small line of hair that went from my chest to my belly button, it would look good. Better than good, it would look fucking awesome. Sean-Connery-James-Bond style. I would take my shirt off at the Isthmus and have women fall all over me just like the guys on *Melrose Place*. I did all my manscaping my very-first night in camp. Nobody knew I completed this model of personal engineering. When to unveil my creation?

The next day we were all on a work party getting the camp ready for the scouts. We had to set -up tents in all the campsites. Midway through it was go time. I did a big over-the-top yawn (like when Bud Bundy would yawn before he put his arms around a babe in *Married With Children*) and simultaneously took off my shirt. Within seconds, the piranhas saw blood in the water.

This is exactly what I did to my chest in a desperate attempt to win girls that summer.

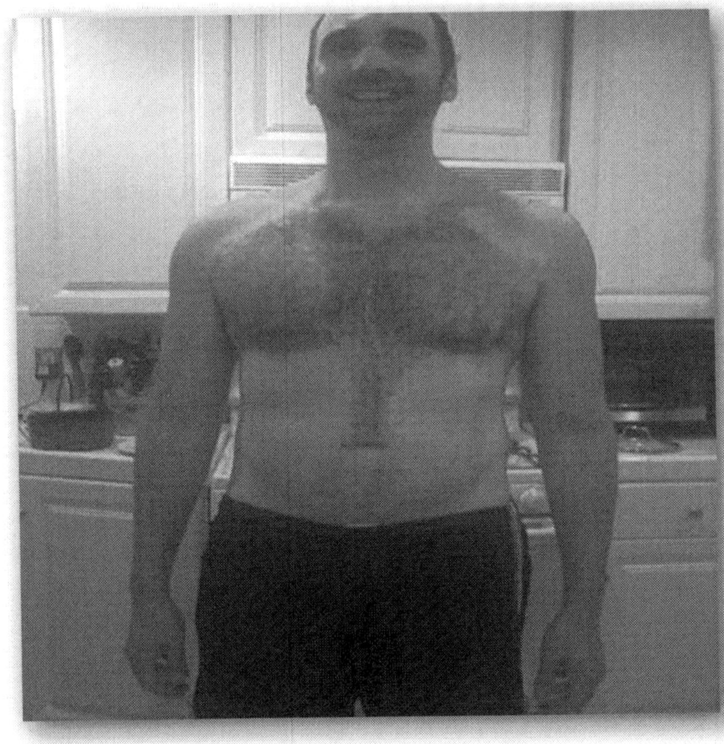

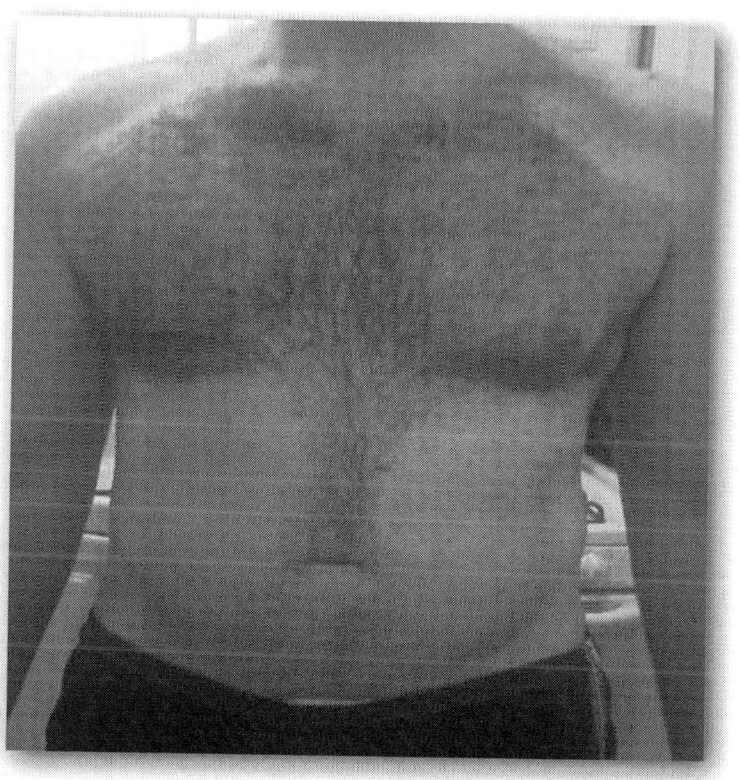

"Jaffe shaved his chest."

"What are you, a chick? Did you shave your vagina as well?"

(*"No, I did not shave my vagina."*)

I was getting laughed at like Carrie on prom night. Time to respond with my own superpower. I didn't have telepathy. Instead I had a perfect lie-alibi.

"Uhm, I didn't shave my chest. This happened while I was diving during a volleyball game."

"AHAAHAHAH" (credibility destroyed).

"Jaffe, you look like a mosquito. No way that fucking happened during a volleyball game."

(It was a long shot.)

"Maybe if you execute a perfect jump serve, it will exfoliate your pores."

"Yeah, will a perfect set to the outside hitter give you dishpan hands?"

The manscape mockery ensued.

Carvillak: "You guys say mosquito. I say it's a big tree."

"Tree."

"Mosquito."

"Mosquitoes, say aye."

"Aye," they said to the twelfth power. It was settled. It was a mosquito.

My ruse was routed. The next day, I scraped the bottom of the Nair barrel and removed what was left of my chest-squito.

All of this was part of my ploy to get girls.

—∾—

I also used tanning oil to look good in my quest to get girls. It was Hawaiian Tropic as I recall, but it was so long ago. How does anyone even remember these things? (Standard bottle, not spray pump. Dark Exotic SPF #6, serial # 372648, but again, it's all such a blur.) On the boat ride to camp I routinely used such an alarming amount of tanning oil that when I laid down on the bow of the boat, I would slide back and forth like a greased-up metronome. The tip of the bow looked like a cookie tin before the dough was laid out. On a side note, my friends in field sports one summer actually used aluminum as a ray catcher and pressure-cooker-tanned themselves in the canyon. Damn, why didn't I think of that? Fully tanned, hairless, and gelled up, I wanted to give Catalina its very-own version of Jersey Shore.

"I hate the ocean, it's all whale sperm. Everybody Google it, because that's why the water is salty, from the f*ckin' whale sperm."

—Snookie "Nicole" Paloozi

Thank you, Snookie, for that thoughtful insight.

If I can turn the conversation away from ejaculating saltwater mammals for a second, I'd like to turn our attention back to where we went out when it was time for action: the Isthmus Bar.

The Isthmus Bar was where we went on our one night off. There was a quick-serve restaurant (Doug's Harbour Reef)

as well as a fancy restaurant that we never went to because money spent on lobstah was money not spent on volume drinking. In between was, and still is, a dance floor with an outdoor bar. It was our *Star Wars* cantina scene, and I was a haphazardly groomed Guido Greedo.

> "Jabba's through with you! He has no use for metrosexuals who drop their chest hair at the first sign of an Isthmus cruise."

My first weekend ever at the Isthmus Bar back in 1992, I watched a guy on staff work his charms with a girl until they went off to the palm trees somewhere out of sight. Then when he came back, the first thing he did was get on the phone (a pay phone) and call his girlfriend and tell her, "There. Now we're even."

Oh my God. Somebody having way more sex than me. Again it was my first summer, and I was taking a self-imposed vow of masturbatory abstinence. I just saw a staff guy go leave and have sex with a girl, and thenhe called his girlfriend back home to say, "Now we're even."

Why he wanted to wreck such a happy relationship that he had with his college girlfriend I had no idea, but the point is this: somebody on staff just got some. According to my calculations, I had to be next.

At our 11:00-hours line of sight, there was a confirmed floozie sighting. We all focused intently. Immediately she grabbed a veteran staff guy, and they went and had quickie sex somewhere off in the bushes.

They were dropping like flies in front of me. Our troops were being yanked away like the marine recon paratroopers in the movie *Aliens*. I felt like Hudson:

"They're coming out of the walls! They're coming out of the God damn walls!"

Again, according to my calculations, I was still next in line. Sexy Isthmus Lady Aliens, abduct me to your romantic getaway spot by the palm trees next to the trash cans and the main road.

(Did I mention romantic?)

It didn't happen. I kept coming back week after week like a modern-day Sisyphus pushing his "Please Have Sex with Me" boulder up the hill. I once was so happy that a girl gave me her phone number that I literally ran down the pier, numbers in hand, screaming, "I got digits!" It was pathetic.

Eventually I discovered I didn't need women to have fun at the Isthmus. This was because "there was another."

The Isthmus Bar has one famous drink: it's called the Buffalo Milk. Many have tried, but I have never seen it recreated successfully. It's the most magical concoction in the world. That drinkwas our leadoff hitter—assuming our leadoff hitter got three hits before the rest of the team made it into the on-deck circle. Post Buffalo Milk we delved into a wide variety of drinks. Everything was right in our wheelhouse.

My Isthmus drinking lineup as a major league batting order with the appropriate baseball player:

1. Buffalo Milk: scrappy leadoff man to get my liver on base (the Lenny Dykstra of alcohol, if you will).
2. 2.zBuffalo Milk again: "Number 2, the captain, Buffalo Milk. Number 2." Thank you, Bob Sheppard.
3. Blue Hawaiian: Sammy Sosa with the White Sox. Limited power, minimal consistency. Still kinda fun to have in the lineup.
4. Long Island Iced Tea: Imagine if Barry Bonds and a Romanian gymnast had a baby, and then that baby grew up and was dating a baseball player who was roided out of his fucking mind.
5. Adios, Motherfucker (Blue Hawaiian with twice the alcohol): Sammy Sosa during the years he used creatine and chewed Flintstone vitamins. Awesome, awesome power; not great in the clutch.
6. Adios, Motherfucker or another Long Island: Pick a Giambi brother here. (Pick the one who hits for power. Not the one who likes strip clubs.)
7. Bud Light: Durable, light, dare I say Steve Finley before he cost my Angels a shot at beating the White Sox in 2005?

Seventh-Inning Stretch—A handful of popcorn from the back bar.

8. Miller Light: Maybe Darin Erstad (solid, edgy, makes ya angry and wanna rabble rouse).
9. Miller Genuine Draft: My man! And one of my all-time favorite players, Milton Motherfucking Bradley!

Alcohol made the Isthmus Bar so much better. To amuse ourselves we'd come up with contests. One night in 1999, a contest was thrown out by my then-girlfriend to see which junior staff member could get the most phone numbers. As a kicker, the numbers needed to be written on them. This contest predated the iPhone craze, and it seemed appropriate at the time. Junior staff ran around like wild banshees as they blindsided yachtees' daughters with demands for their phone numbers so they could call them to start a romance once the summer was over. There these kids were getting numbers for a contest, all the while getting marked-up like Guy Pearce in *Memento.*

Whenever we found junior staff that drank themselves sick, Clint and I would play long arm of the law.

Cue the *Bad Boys* music from the opening of *COPS.*

It was time to play Good Cop, Bad Lieutenant.

Clint: "So John and Pedro thought they would drink some tonight and get housed. Well, that seemed like a pretty good idea, UNTIL YOU GOT CAUGHT!"

My time to shine.

"Here you guys are, you're sick, vomiting from all the alcohol, and I have just one question for you: Who wants a glass of hot dog water with a shot of mayonnaise?"

Back to Clint the Good Cop: "YOU GUYS ARE GONNA BE UP TOMORROW MORNING RUNNING LAPS AROUND CAMP, AND THAT'S ASSUMING YOU DON'T GET FIRED AND SENT HOME, WHICH WILL PROBABLY HAPPEN ANYWAY!"

(Hmm, our Good Cop may in fact be a Bad Cop.)

My turn again:

"John and Pedro: I know you guys are sick. And I know you feel bad for drinking all that alcohol. So what we're going to do is this: we're going to get you guys some more alcohol and some canned anchovies. Also, they sell clam juice in the general store. Is that OK? Are you guys ever gonna drink again?"

John and Pedro (between vomiting and crying): "No, no! We're sorry! We'll never drink again! *PLEASE DON'T FIRE US*!"

You know that phrase, "Absolute power corrupts absolutely"? Well, that phrase should read, "Absolute power is absolutely fucking awesome."

As we left the Isthmus one magical evening after a smorgasbord of cocktails far more magical than anything served at

Hogwarts, we noticed it was a yachtee weekend. There were giant signs hung up everywhere. This meant we had to have one. McBrayer and I ran back. We grabbed onta a giant sign that went from palm tree to palm tree across the walkway into the Isthmus in full view of everybody. It didn't matter. We knew they couldn't see us. The two of us were running a covert Black Ops mission with everything except some sweet-ass night vision goggles like the ones I use when I watch the *Paris Hilton Sex Tape* video.

> "Strap one on the sign is down! Repeat, strap one is down!"
>
> "Strap two has fallen!"
>
> "Losing control of strap three! Strap four is all that remains between us and the OH Wait. Oh no. Oh boy, it's uhm, the uhm, sheriff and, uhm, I think he, uhm, sees uhhh…yes, sir. We aren't taking the sign. No, sir. We are putting it back right now, immediately."

The sheriff at the Isthmus probably had bigger fish to fry than two camp punks on a sign-stealing rampage. However, he was there to lay down the long arm of the law. My favorite story of a camp staffer getting in trouble with the sheriff at Catalina was a few summers prior. One of the guys went into the general store and started switching the prices from certain items and placing them on the alcohol. Talk about market-price fixation. Our camp had its very-own Gordon Gekko, and Jose Cuervo was his Anacot Steel. Interestingly enough, he wasn't arrested…just severely reprimanded. Then he cried and cried, swearing he wouldn't drink anymore because drinking made him do stupid things. What a pussy.

Sans signs, McBrayer and I headed back to the end of the docks. Normally we took the shuttle back to camp but not tonight. Tonight we had a private boat, and it was headed by (drum roll, please) Davonte. That's right. My favorite original gangsta had island fever, and now he owned his very own boat. Let Tupac know we found the California Love Boat. For what it's worth, today this OG gangsta can't get enough of Facebook. Time for Farmville bitchez!

We stumbled onto the pier. All of us. Clint, Allen, McBrayer, myself, and, of course, Davonte. We had to make it back to his little boat because it was time to go. Plus we were pretty sure he had MGD on the boat, and that sounded awesome. By the way, in Davonte's drinking lineup, the one-to-nine hitters were all beer. MGD, rinse, repeat. The ten-to-eighteen hitters followed suit.

We flew and fell into each other. I walked sideways into Clint while falling face first.

> "Watch where you're going, Clint, you fucking asshole!"
>
> "Seriously? You just fell into me Jaffe."
>
> Allen: "Oh, well, *HOW CONVENIENT*."

It was time to ask Davonte the serious questions about his brand-new nautical whip.

> "Hey, Davonte, is there a stripper pole on your boat?"
>
> "Do we do drive-bys from port or from starboard?"
>
> "How many rap video ho's will be accompanying us on this fantastic voyage?"
>
> "Jaffe, did you get digits tonight?"
>
> "Shut up!"

A cacophony of crazy crew stumbled onto Davonte's boat. We were all climbing into the cooler for some of that sweet, sweet MGD. (It's the champagne of beers, people. Recognize!) Then all of a sudden, we heard a loud, booming, and, unfortunately, totally serious voice.

> "Gentlemen, is one of you sober enough to drive this boat?"

At the time I remember thinking McBrayer was talking and wanting to look at him and say something horrible and offensive, possibly about his mother. For some unknown reason, I refrained.

We turned and looked.

There he was: Sheriff Brubaker had followed us down the pier.

What the, why would he? It made no sense.

Just because we were rampantly drunk loons about to board our vessel (Huh huh, he said vessel), did that give him cause to shadow us? Probably so, but that's not the point.

We heard the question again, sending panic through our senses.

> "Gentlemen, is one of you sober enough to drive this boat?"

Davonte stepped up to talk to the sheriff.

Of all the people to use as our United Nations delegate, I was pretty sure this was the worst member. I don't think the president of Syria is the one you want telling the UN Security Council that the Arab Spring is a peaceful protest and the army is there solely for moral support.

Davonte stepped up. It was his moment to shine.

> "Officer, I'm sorry. This is my boat here. I am totally sober. My friends have had a few drinks, but I am taking them back to camp so they can go straight to bed. Also here are my running lights as well as all my life preservers. Is there anything else I can help you with this evening?"

Buford T. Justice looked us over…

> "OK, fine. You gentlemen are free to go."

Holy shit. It worked. He bought it. Davonte passed with flying colors. He had sobered up on the spot, and now he was starting his boat.

We left the Isthmus in utter silence. No one dared to speak. Our boat journeyed out of the bay with the same eerie quiet as the *Erebus* that was looking for Kurtz in *Apocalypse Now.* I played the role of Willard, with only the thoughts in my head to keep me company.

"Boy Scout camp was close, real close. I couldn't see it yet, but I could feel it, as if the boat was being sucked upriver and the water was flowing back into the Isthmus. Whatever was going to happen, it wasn't gonna be the way they call it back in Emerald Bay."

Once we broke the harbor, Davonte turned and looked at us, unblinking. Then a smile emerged out of the corner of his mouth.

> "You guys are all bitchez. I fucking had you going, didn't I? Didn't I, motherfuckers! I swear to God, don't fucking worry, I got this. Now pass me a fucking MGD. Let's get our drink on."

Whenever we went to the Isthmus Bar, Clint had an anthem for us all. He used to parody the great *Married with Children* bit of "At the Nudie Bar."

If you remember, Al takes Bud to the Nudie Bar and regales him with poetic verse. Herein were Clint's best lines:

1.> At the Isthmus Bar
Where you meet a cute chick,
and she might suck your dick
At the Isthmus Bar
2.> At the Isthmus Bar,
After week six
They're all cute chicks
At the Isthmus Bar

—ɤɤ—

These were our top-five favorite songs to listen to at the Isthmus Bar.

Clarence Carter—"Strokin'"

Jimmy Buffet—"Margaritaville" (obviously)

Right Said Fred—"I'm Too Sexy" (accompanying gay pride choreographed dance maneuvers mandatory)

Billy Ray Cyrus—"Friends in Low Places" (accompanying gay pride line dance maneuvers mandatory)

Glenn Miller—"In the Mood"

XIII

Scaring the Kids

The Five Biggest Fears You Have Working at Summer Camp:

1.) Ghosts
2.) Alien abduction
3.) Accidentally desecrating sacred Indian burial grounds
4.) Getting stranded in the wilderness and actually having to use your wilderness survival merit badge skills
5.) Being confronted by pretty girls and actually having to talk to them

Nothing is better than scaring little kids. I learned this in 1990 when I was a Provisional Scout at another Boy Scout camp: Camp Whitsett in the High Sierras. As a Provisional, or Provo Scout, I was in a campsite with nine other kids my age and no adult supervision whatsoever. (Gentlemen, let the inmates police the asylum themselves.) One of the kids there was really into *Nightmare on Elm Street* movies. He was into them so much that he wanted us to call him…wait for it… you'll never guess…that's right! He wanted us to call him Freddy. Well, "Freddy," as he liked to be called, was batshit fucking crazy. He got bored one day and proceeded to shoot at us with his handheld BB gun as we jumped between tents. Freddy would also grab two bamboo sticks so that he could spar with somebody he knew would lose. That somebody was me. Freddy, as I was about to find out repeatedly, was really good at martial arts. If Freddy was my sensei, then I was the cricket that got the shit whacked out of him. (On a side note: so much fun!) I was the karate fighter who needed to taste his own blood to get motivated. Then I went out and got my ass kicked again. And again.

I asked Freddy if he knew how to use ninja stars.

> "They're called shuriken, Seth, and yes, I do know how to use them."

(Stupid question on my part. God, why was I always asking stupid questions?)

I continued.

"Well, Freddy, could you use one, you know, to hurt somebody or something?"

> "Seth, do you see that guy walking over there on the other side of the lake?"

I squinted my eyes.

"Well, I could hit him in the temple. That would kill him, Seth. Do you understand? That's why I didn't bring my throwing stars to camp."

"Uh-huh."

Freddy wasn't just about channeling his inner most extreme ninja. He also explained to me how if you laid back on your bed and listened to Pink Floyd's *Dark Side of the Moon*, you would be transported into the fifth dimension and youcould relive any experience you wanted. (Is there anything that album can't do?) Freddy's favorite experience was reliving the time he lost his virginity to his girlfriend Kelly, who, according to Freddy, was totally beautiful, and they did it no less than one hundred times.

I tried the *Dark Side of the Moon* experiment when I returned home that summer with the hope that I could travel into the fifth dimension and relive watching Freddy have sex with Kelly. I waited until 97.1 KLSX was playing a Pink Floyd song, "Another Brick in the Wall" (yes, I know, it's from another album) and then I jumped on my bed and closed my eyes and tried to visualize myself in the fifth dimension. Also, and this was very important, Freddy let me know that there were evil demons and bad people in the fifth dimension, so you needed a weapon with you. It had to be at your side or holstered to your ankle. With my Swiss Army knife in tow, I proceeded to try and teleport myself into a magical dimension while little British schoolchildren railed on and on about not getting their pudding (or any royalties).

"A dimension of sight and sound."

(A dimension where I could watch Kelly having sex.)

It didn't work.

Well, that was after camp. This was during camp. Back to scaring children.

Freddy also had the full Freddy Krueger ensemble. Didn't see that plotline developing, did you?

One night, we hatched a plan.

Freddy would wait on one side of the bushes in full gear. On the other side were the nine of us, trying not to laugh. Then, as a couple of younger scouts approached and got within range, nine of us would jump up and start yelling at the two kids. If, by the way, you're wondering about our credibility here, remember what I said in Chapter I. When you're ten years old, the smartest person you will ever meet is a teenager. We were teenagers!

The kids approached.

We all jumped up in unison.

"You guys gotta' get out of here!"

"Holy shit, we saw Freddy Krueger!"

"He's coming and he likes small scouts. Anybody that hasn't hit his second class needs to run!"

Cue the villain.

Freddy jumped up and started running. The other nine of us would run in separate directions, screaming, paying no mind whatsoever to the kids we were scaring. It was masterful.

And then we got caught.

Turns out one of the kids we scared didn't go tell his scoutmaster. Oh, no! Way worse. This kid did the unspeakable. He went and called his mom from the pay phone. Then she demanded to speak with the scoutmaster. That made sense since *THEY WERE GETTING A DIVORCE.*

Heads were gonna roll.

The staff at Whitsett told the troop they sent Freddy home. In fact, that's not what happened at all. They were so amused at the story that they laughed it off and just made him unload milk crates and supplies for a couple of days. Also they asked him to stop using the nickname Freddy so as to keep up the appearances that he'd been thrown out of camp. Our Freddy had to change back to his real name, and then that kid's troop actually extended an olive branch. (That was funny since we instigated everything.) They invited us into their campsite and we all went over for a peace offering: peach cobbler between our Provisional Scouts and the victims we traumatized.

All good, right…just make sure you don't break character. After all, we sent home the Nightmare from Elm Street.

"Hey, Freddy, do you want some cobbler?"

"Shut up. It's Mike. And yeah, I do want cobbler."

"Oh, OK Freddy, I mean *Mike*."

—⁓—

When I arrived at Emerald Bay, I had some extensive on-the-job training in the field of shock-and-fright schadenfreude.

The first lesson I received on scaring kids happened one day when I was sitting around with some scouts. I was an innocent bystander for that one. In 1992, I was teaching the cooking merit badge, and Alphonzo stopped by to visit. Alphonzo was a cook in the kitchen and an incredibly smart kid. He would be leaving for UC–Davis the following year. Alphonzo sat down to talk to the kids about the value of scouting. Cooking merit badge is a good class for beginner scouts, hence a class full of impressionable ten-to-twelve-year olds. I was sitting there with ten- to-twelve-year-old kids flipping burgers and talking about action movies, when Alphonso felt the need to give the kids a very important public service announcement. Why, I have no idea. Here is Alphonzo's speech because, just like Randy Watson ("Randy Watson!"), he believes the children are our future. Oh, and by the way, it was maybe the worst speech ever made at summer camp.

> "You kids need to know that you need to be good scouts because you don't want to go to prison and get Christmas treed like El Japo in *American Me*."

Wow. That went horribly wrong. We were all speechless. Not quite how I wanted to scare kids, although I have to say, it did work.

—~—

The lifesaving class practiced CPR training on the dining hall porch in the evenings. They would lay down Resusci-Anne. Resusci -Anne was a plastic doll that you would breathe into to work on your cadence when you were getting CPR certified. We called her Bitch-in-a-Box. Resusci- Anne was there so the kids could practice saving a drowning plastic doll's life. I knew this. I also knew how to climb underneath the dining hall porch and traverse the crawl space like I was Willem Dafoe in *Platoon*. I went around the side. Then I crawled under the entire dining hall patio. All of a sudden, I was perfectly placed under Resusci-Anne…waiting for the right moment.

The next kid was called up to practice on her.

"Scott Jenkinsen, troop 902."

As he leaned down to practice his CPR, I yelled:

"No, please! Don't do it! I'm alive! I don't need CPR! I'm gonna make it!"

Scout jumps back, scared. Scout hears me laughing. It was awesome!

Now I was an adrenaline junkie. Who was the next victim of 'Camp Scare Tactics?'

—~—

The maintenance staff caught a rattlesnake in camp. Instead of killing the snake with a shovel or a shotgun, or a little of column A and column B, they opted to throw Ol' Snakey into the freezer. As we walked down to lunch, they pulled out the frozen solid snake and threw it down on the back table outside the dining hall.

Thunk! It was rock solid.

We stared at the snake. It was not moving.

As we watched, I started talking. As a college sophomore, I was seen as being semi-intelligent.

"You guys know they hibernate, right?"

A collective "Yeah."

"So it's just sleeping."

"Yeah."

"They're not warm-blooded. I know because I'm the Nature Director."

Slowly I reached for a small stick. Small enough to fit through the opening between the planks where the snake was situated.

"In fact, it could wake up at any sec..."

BAM!

I jammed the stick straight up. It went between the two planks and hit the snake in its midsection. The snake flew up into the air. It literally got high enough into the air to make direct eye contact with one of the junior staff sitting at the table. He jumped. The rest of them jumped. I fell over laughing.

The best part about scaring other people was that there was no way the karma would ever come back to get me. That's not how karma works at all.

—⁓—

It was 1999 and Dillon had something he wanted to show us. Dillon was part of our inner circle. He was very quiet, which contrasted with his imposing physical presence. He also had a goatee and angry blond hair that made him look like an extra in *Sons of Anarchy*. We went up into Dillon's cabin. It was me, Dillon, Clint, and Allen. What could it be?

There it was, a bootleg copy of *The Blair Witch Project*.

We all froze. We'd been at camp all summer. Somebody had brought out a director's screener one Saturday night, but we were all at the Isthmus Bar. Now on a Tuesday night, on Dillon's crappy little TV, we had a chance to watch this movie.

The debate started.

"Is it just a movie?"

"I thought it was a documentary based on what actually happened to them."

"It might be the raw footage."

"Didn't you see the interviews with their parents on the ScyFy Channel and all the missing reward info?"

"It's totally real."

We'd spent the entire summer putting down Blair Witch mementoes everywhere in camp. And this was before we even saw the movie. Bags of sticks and hanging bones were the norm in front of cabins andthe A-Frames. Parts of our camp were decorated like a Blair Witch Christmas tree.

Real or not, we'd whipped ourselves into a frenzy. It was time to watch some grainy handheld video of two guys and a girl in a forest… (a different kind of grainy handheld video of two guys and a girl in the forest).

The movie started at 9:30 p.m. At 11:00 p.m., we were all breathless and scared out of our minds.

We bought it.

Everybody who lived on the hill was going to bed. I had to turn and march all the way back through camp and toward my A-Frame. McBrayer jumped up as well. He was in the 3rd A-Frame. I was in the 4th.

"Come on, let's go Seth."

"Yeah dude, I'm like super tired."

My hands were shaking from being so nervous. My eyes were racing back and forth. I was not tired. I was not tired.

We walked fast. It felt like the trees were watching our every movement. Each step was so loud, I could only assume it was awakening the ghosts of scouts who had been lost during wilderness-survival-merit-badge training.

We finally hit McBrayer's A-frame.

> "Hey, dude. If you want to swing back to my A-Frame and hang out, it's cool."
>
> "No, Seth. I'm good. Going to sleep."

I was on my own. The walk resumed. It was less than five hundred yards to my A-Frame. That was fifteen hundred feet, which was roughly seven hundred and fifty steps, which I was literally counting one at a time. I also kept stopping and turning around, convinced that I was being followed. In the back of my head, I thought about all the things we said to the kids in wilderness-survival-merit-badge class before they spent the night in the woods.

> "Don't make a lot of noise after 10:00 p.m. That's when the night cobras like to move around."
>
> "There used to be an insane asylum on the other side of camp. After the jailbreak five years ago, they shut it down. I think they caught most of them. Oh well, you kids have fun tonight."

Hell, we even told kids at the opening night campfire about a crazy Vietnam vet in the mountains who lived off of the wild goats he caught and broke off his back. His name was Harvey C. Paulsen, and some of the veterans on staff had actually seen him running along the ridgeline after a goat, which he then caught in one fell swoop and snapped in half over his knee. (During the PC era I assumed they would make

Harvey C. Paulsen a vegan Occupy Wall Street protester who railed against the 1percent% of scouts who got their Eagle Scout, but that was not the case.)

I also thought about every stupid prank call I'd made on the camp phones to other people in their A-frames.

Ring, ring

"Hello."

"Go check on the children."

"You're an idiot, Seth. The camp phones are supposed to be used for emergencies only."

"It is an emergency. You need to go check on the children."

"Good-bye, Seth!"

I stopped dead cold in my tracks. Surrounded in darkness, adrenaline coursing through my blood a mile a minute, terrified for dear life, it was all coming together. What if the Blair Witch and her long-lost cousins, Freddy Krueger and Jason, were working together at this very moment with the escapees from the insane asylum to fill my A-Frame with night cobras? Impossible? I kept breathing faster and louder. Then I took off running as fast as I could.

A dramatic reenactment of what was going through my head at that exact moment:

Feet were kicking up dust. They probably already finished off the scouts and scoutmasters, so now it was up to me to save myself. I couldn't worry about them anyway. The children were weak, and they would only slow me down. If I could just barricade myself in my A-frame, I knew I would be safe. I could feel them chasing me, their hands about to descend on my neck and swallow my soul.

If the boogeyman and the Blair Witch demanded an opening and used the scouts as hostages, I didn't care. I don't negotiate with phantom soul spectre terrorists. Have all the scouts you want. I'm saving myself tonight.

I made it into my A-Frame unharmed. Turned on all the lights and paced for a few minutes (read: for about an hour), and then passed out. In the morning I woke up and looked directly outside. Everything appeared normal. I stepped out of my A-frame, and suddenly I felt squishing between my toes.

Oh my God. It had to be a dead body. The Blair Witch left me a scout from astronomy class to let me know that I was next. It was a Sicilian astronomical message!

I looked down, readying my eyes to see the corpse. All I saw was twisted red, some parts with substance, and then I inspected closely and…I…saw…pepperoni.

I had been involved in an ongoing prank war that summer with the entire kitchen staff. Very cleverly, they snuck up early that morning and dropped pizza on my front door.

In exchange for me leaving violated fake plastic dolls in their freezer and stealing their hidden ice cream stash, they saw fit to place a special order of leftover Saturday pizza on my doorstep. They did this hoping to get wild animals to eat food outside my A-frame and make noise, but it actually worked out better than they'd imagined. I'd survived the Blair Witch and all her mysterious counterparts, only to be waylaid by stale camp pizza, which I thought was a dead body.

XIV

Porn

My Top Five Naked Scenes in a Summer Camp Movie (help from celebritymoviearchive.com):

1.) America Olivo in the *Friday the 13th* remake
2.) Kristi Ducati in *Meatballs IV*
3.) Tania Mero and Kaye Penaflor in *Friday the 13th, Part 10*, aka *Jason X* (yes, it take place in outer space, but I'm still counting it)
4.) Kate French in *Fired Up*
5.) Fabiana Udenio in *Summer School**

*She's not naked, but that's OK here. Still worked for preteen Seth Jaffe. Still works now.

In the days before the iPad and the Internet machine, everybody on staff had to have some sort of porn. It was a long summer. (My God, we're not Catholic priests here, people… this is a good thing.)

We needed porn because we were stuck on an island all summer, and some of us (read: this guy) weren't having sex. Ironically I didn't utilize porn until my fifth summer on staff. Prior to becoming a director, I was petrified of getting caught whacking it. This was because in my first summer at camp, on the very-first week, they caught a kid named Jackson.

For the next three weeks kids on staff would say, "Let's play a game." Then they would hold one hand open while pounding down the other hand as a fist like they were playing Rock, Paper, Scissors. Except they would say:

"Rock, Paper, Jackson."

No way was I going to be included in that game. I actually went the entire summer without taking care of myself. It was ironic that I couldn't last twenty-four hours in a bet I made a few summers later. Either way, I knew that as a director I was above reproach from being criticized for having a secret stash. I soon noticed that porn was like alcohol. Everybody on the director staff kept some.

I even used porn for a very-special purpose one evening. It was 11:55 p.m., and our good buddy, Nilius, was about to turn eighteen. He would no longer be classified as a minor. This meant we had to wake him up and indoctrinate him into the magical world of adult cinema.

At exactly midnight, we burst into his cabin, and started shaking Nilius and turning the lights in his cabin on and off. Then I put a lighter up to the smoke detector to get some background birthday music.

"Wake up, bitch. It's your birthday. We've got plans for..."

Baaa Waaaw! Baaa Waaaaw! Baaa Waaaaw!

Nilius, dazed and sleepy, didn't want to wake up. Just then, Allen, who was in Nilius's cabin, jumped up and, like Belushi in *Animal House* going after the guitar, he took a broom and beat the smoke detector to death.

Baa Waaaw! Baa Waaaw! Baa Crash. Whack Whack Whack.

The smoke detector was on its last legs. Just like the Terminator, his little red light was about to go out. Allen gave it one last whack and then went straight back to bed as though nothing had happened. Nilius was sufficiently summoned.

A time-honored tradition at camp was the director movie night. Once a week we would all congregate in the staff lounge and watch a nudie movie.

"Come on, Nilius. Wake up. You're eighteen now, and you need to go experience your first director movie night."

"No, I don't think so. I don't really like that kind of stuff anyway. It degrades women."

"HAAHAHAHAHAHAHAAH."

"Let's go, bitch. We're on the move."

Our selection for that evening was relatively tame. We were watching *Cum Guzzling Felch Fuckers Volume VIII.* (We never watched that movie, but I did read the book.) Actually, the only director movie I had was one that hadn't been debuted until this special moment. It was *The Jenny McCarthy Playmate of the Year* video.

I realize that nowadays, the world of porn has evolved faster than the Hanta virus in stagnant village water. Jason Kaplan from the great *Howard Stern Show* talks about wrapping his iPhone in double plastic wrap and taking it into the shower to watch porn. Well that's all well and good, but this was 1996, and it was well before the magical days of waterproof aquatic 'Bang Bus' viewing. A number of people nowadays will tell you that *Playboy* doesn't even count as porn. Years ago, when my buddy Drazen was a stand-up comic, he used to say:

"'I'm so desensitized to porn that the only way I can feel anything is if I see two Chinese nuns licking a yak ass."

I've even read articles in *Playboy*, or at least the cartoons.

We placed Nilius on the center couch and loaded up the videocassette (1996, people). It was time to watch some good old-fashioned Chinese-nun-yak-ass porn. Over the next sixty minutes, we followed Jenny McCarthy as she pumped water naked from a fountain and did laundry, also while naked. She talked about her *Playboy* experience and what it meant to be the PMOY. Then she warned us that she would go on to become a social activist as well as a close friend and confidant of Oprah.

Nilius, tired and mildly traumatized, went off to bed. We didn't think anything of his special evening until we realized he was at every future director movie night, front row center. His perfect attendance record told us one thing: we had created a monster. Nilius went on to love porn so much that he invented a personal rule for himself: he would no longer masturbate on Sundays so as to stem the flow.

I once asked Nilius about his No-Palm Sunday rule.

> "What if there's nobody around, and you saw a commercial with a bunch of hot models?"
>
> "Nope. Not on Sunday."
>
> "You see some hotties at the gym and they're, I don't know, for argument's sake, just lifting weights in sports bras and Arizona State University regulation-issued butt shorts, and spanking each other and rubbing hot oil all over themselves while they put 'em on the glass, and then you go home and then it's OK?"
>
> "Sunday, no. Maybe Monday."
>
> "Can you at least have sex with a girl on Sundays, or are you like Chick Won't Fill-Lay? Ha-ha."

Unfazed, Nilius pointed out, "Nope, dude. Sex is OK. Just no other stuff."

> "OK, Nilius. What if you're watching Internet porn on Saturday night and it's close to midnight and the clip runs over?"
>
> "It's cool, dude. That's OK."

Aha! Legal loophole.

It's like Damon Wayans said in the appropriately titled *The Last Boy Scout:* "Yeah, a security system. And I circumvented it."

I wanted to take credit for inventing director movie night, but in fact, it had been around since the beginning of camp, or at least the eighties. I just made director movie night incredibly popular and somewhat of an unhealthy obsession for the over-eighteen-year-olds on staff. This in turn probably hurt their ability to form meaningful relationships with women in the future, but hey, that's what friends at camp are for, right?

—∿—

When it was time for a director movie, or a DM as we affectionately called it, I was like Jamie Kennedy in the movie *Scream.*

"People, listen up. There are rules to a director movie."

On cue, somebody would always ask:

"Seth, can you explain the rules again?"

"You mean you people don't know?"

"No. We don't know."

"Rule number one: You have to say anything that's on your mind, period! If we're watching *The*

> *Black Butt Sisters do Baltimore* or *Anal Cuties of China Town* and you have something to say, you need to let it be said. The more commentary the better, people."

Examples of comments made during previous director movies:

> "I hope they're married. Otherwise they're sinners."
>
> "Does he love her? If he doesn't love her, my heart's not in this either."
>
> "You guys can't tell because you can't see that guy's hand, but he's got a class ring from Johns Hopkins. He was in my civics class."

I wanted the director movie experience to be like IMAX for the ears. I wanted it to rival seeing *Bad Boys* in an inner-city movie theatre in Baltimore.

> "Girl, look at his chest!"
>
> "Oh my gawd, girlfriend. Will Smif is so fine."
>
> "Yo, those motherfuckers are getting fucked up!"
>
> "Rule number two: This is a No-Beating Zone. If you wish to take care of business, you need to leave the premises."

All of a sudden, one of our staff members, Ralph, stood up.

> "Are you going somewhere, buddy?"

> "Yeah, I am! I think it's bullshit that I can't whip it out here. I don't want to watch the movie and follow all your stupid fucking rules."
>
> "Wow, OK. We'll miss you, buddy."

Rule number two was what kept us from becoming really, really creepy. Serial killers watch porn together without this rule in place. Not us.

There would be an introduction to the movie before we hit play on the VCR. I prided myself on the introduction because there was a historic theatre in Baltimore called The Senator that did something similar to this back in the day.

> "Gentlemen, today's Oscar-winning piece hails from the lovely cinematic region of Chatsworth, California. The actors are a girl with daddy issues, a stripper, and a dancer who doesn't like to be called a stripper. It also stars Peter North."
>
> "*Y*AAAAHH!"
>
> ("And there was a little too much rejoicing.")

We were all fans of the man we affectionately called Pedro Norte.

One fine Wednesday evening, five minutes after our movie started and we were all settled in, there was a knock on the door.

No fucking way! All the scouts, the scoutmasters, and the kids were in bed.

We specifically started director movies after all the scouts were secured in their campsites and safely asleep. There's no way we were about to get caught here.

The door opened, and a small scout in his jacket asked in a mousy little voice:

"Have you seen my ranger?"

Holy shit! We were watching *Reverse Double Blowbang Soccer Moms*, and now we had a traumatized child in front of us. This was not good. Start booking this kid's therapy sessions. And send us all to jail like we're a Penn State defensive coordinator.

Suddenly the little kid stood up. It was Brock. He was a nineteen-year-old on staff and currently attending UCSB. (U Cock-Sucking Bastard!)

We were too scared to even blink. Then he started laughing at us like Pesci in *Goodfellas*.

"I had you. I fucking had you, and you all fell for it."

To this day if I go up to Brock and ask him if he's seen his ranger, it gets an awesome response.

Here is a matrix of each person on staff and their porn of choice:

Name	Stash
Seth	I owned the aforementioned Jenny McCarthy video. In later summers, I brought two cassettes to camp that stood out. One was called *The Dinner Party,* and the other was called *Two Fucking Hours. Two Fucking Hours* was a personal favorite for the following reason: "Hey, guys, what do you want to do for the next two fucking hours?" "I don't know. I've got two fucking hours to kill." Oh, the hilarity!
Clint	Clint had a Jansport bag full of nudie magazines. To lift the bag you practically needed a spotter. I've moved dead hookers from the trunk of my car into the basement that weighed less than this bag.

Davonte's older brother Jorge	George had the Pam and Tommy Lee tape. This was the holy grail of sex tapes. It's Oscar-worthy in its handheld, grainy glory. There's even a shout-out to Catalina Island when they're on the boat.
Allen	Had an actual girlfriend who visited from time to time. In between visits, he was like a camel.
Waterfront Staff	Actual sex with actual women (hate them so much!).

It was a long summer. We needed porn to keep our sanity, otherwise we might have turned out like Jack Nicholson in *The Shining,* chasing around the scouts while brandishing our Swiss Army knives. Look, I know that none of the staff at Vacation Bible Summer Camp or Band Camp had a secret porn stash. It was probably just us. Thank God!

XIV

Broomball

Five Best Sports to Play at Summer Camp:

1.) Broomball
2.) Capture the Flag
3.) Kayak Football
4.) Ultimate Frisbee
5.) Scoutmaster Belly-flop Competition (so many qualified applicants)

Broomball was the most important event at camp. It was our Hunger Games. If your staff could somehow win a broomball title, you had bragging rights not just for the summer, but for every other summer you ever served on camp staff. You could pull the old-timers' move and talk about how your Waterfront team from 1994 would have demolished the 2002 Scoutrcraft team that won the title. To quote Bill Walton, "These are men, competing for the ultimate prize."

There was a trophy as well. It was a Stanley Cup-replica trophy made out of aluminum and balsa wood, 1/25 the size of the actual cup. And it was beautiful in all its glory.

Broomball was brought to camp in 1994. It was a one-night, winner-take-all event, and each area would constitute a team. Leftover people, such as the maintenance staff, would go to a smaller team, maybe handicraft staff.

1994: We arrived at the dining hall early. I wasn't known for being early to anything, and even when I was, I still was dogged by criticism. Per the PC TaskMaster:

"You know, Seth, early is on time and on time is late."

Well, by God, if broomball started at 8:00 p.m., then I was going to get there incredibly early I was so excited. (OK, so it was 8:02—not bad.)

The tables inside the dining hall were all on their sides and turned inward in the shape of a hockey rink. To further simulate an actual hockey rink, they had laid down flour for the red line, the blue line, and the white lines (hahahaha). This is what the broomball court looked like with both teams.

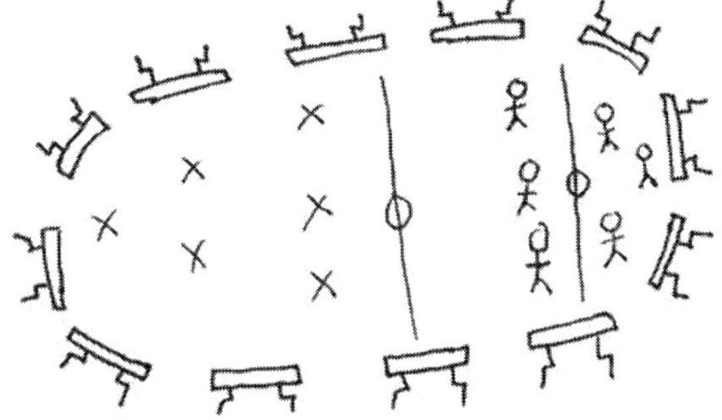

I looked around. Different guys on staff were running around like Comanche Indians at a buffalo hunt, holding their brooms in the air. The Waterfront staff were all wearing customized black life jackets. They whacked each other with their brooms to test the strength of their broomball-proof vests.

"Thank you, sir, may I have another one!"

Whack!

"Hit me again. It doesn't hurt."

Whack! Whack!

"*HIT ME AGAIN*!"

The rangers were putting on eye black. They were also marking their arms with their ubiquitous red *R* for Rangers.

All we needed were the two guys from the movie *The Program* to spit into each other's mouths and utter:

"I'm gonna bust your gut and watch you die!"

Then our camp director got on the microphone to explain the rules to our broomball bloodsport.

> "Everybody, listen up because I'm only saying this once. Here are the rules. There are two ten-minute halves. Whoever scores the most goals wins the game

and advances to play the next team. At the end of the night, there will be a champion."

Wow. OK. Nothing mentioned about fighting. Nothing about slashing or checking or cross-checking.

I better check myself before I wreck myself. ("Cuz broomball goals is bad for yo' health, son.")

The first two teams were called. It was not us. We were spectators. The rangers were taking on Field Sports. Take the rangers in this one going away. Immediately the regulation-issued broomball (a lacrosse ball coated in duct tape) was off and flying. Much like the Golden Snitch in *Harry Potter*, the broomball was seemingly left alone. That was because there was a free-for-all of people trying to check each other into the boards. All of a sudden, one of the rangers was caught napping and checked while he was looking the other way, andthen he went over the table with a marvelous crash.

BamBamBamBam!

I looked outside the dining hall. The scouts were all lined-up outside, hitting the windows like it was game seven. Chants of "Hit 'em!" and "Fight!" rang through the dining hall from the scouts who wanted blood.

The ranger who fell came back into play. It was all happening so fast. The ball flipped the other way. Field Sports had a breakaway. One man and the goal.

Boom! Side check. Field Sports is down. Repeat, Field Sports is down.

The ball went the other way. Rangers had the ball. Red R's on their arms breezed past the Field Sports defense.

Allen shoots, he scores!

Goal number one was on the books. Rangers 1–Field Sports 0.

After twenty minutes the rangers had prevailed, 5–3.

"Next up: Waterfront versus NatureStaff."

It was our turn. Not only was it our turn, but we had drawn the number-one seed in the tournament: the Waterfront staff. They were a pretty-boy goon squad, all of them built like Adonis and trained to destroy, like Kurt Russell in *Soldier* or Brad Pitt in *Troy*.

Our team had one terrible athlete who played some college volleyball. That was me. I was one of our best players.

"Fwww!!!"

The whistle blew and we were off.

The ball skated past on my left. Then it was on my right. I took a good whack and lost my broom. As I went for my broom by the boards, the Kobra Kai sent their sweep-the-leg hit squad after me. It wasn't so much a broomball game out there as it was an unscripted smackdown of your opponents. Each and every broomball player was looking to deliver a bounty on somebody like he was part of the New Orleans Saints defense.

CRASH!

I went hurtling into the boards. Good thing I decided to wear Tevas to broomball. I'm sure that's what Mark Messier used to support the blades on his skates when he was winning all those Stanley Cups. Off I was running again. It was too late. By isolating me and scaring the rest of the people, the Waterfront staff scored a goal. The Nature staff taught kids how to identify mammals. We taught them which types of rocks came from magma versus plate tectonics. We weren't like the Waterfront staff who played football and water polo and trained like Drago at the imperial Russian Mountainside Fortress in Siberia. After the Waterfront staff powered their way forward and scored a goal, the air horn sounded.

HAAWWWNNNKKK!

Then again.

And again and again.

Leonidas and the Spartans stepped over their first batch of piled Persian dead.

We were that dead pile.

The Waterfront staff went on to win the inaugural broomball tournament in a landslide. On a side note, one of the cooks in the kitchen was checked into the boards so hard that it triggered a minor heart attack, and he had to go to the big hospital. This only added to the broomball legend.

In 1995, we lost again.

In 1996 it was my first year as a director. Jake was on the team as well. He was a renowned hothead who would snap during flag football games on the beach if a play didn't work out well. Our very-own Kyle Turley. Nothing like throwing a combustible player on a bad team into the mix. Not only was

I team captain this time, but I was determined to break the Nature curse. We'd never even scored a goal, let alone made it out of the first round. The North Texas Mean Green had experienced more tournament success than we had.

Our first opponent:

The Field Sports staff and my good buddy Carvillak. Clint was also on his team. My eyes narrowed in focus. So did Jake's eyes, which were burning red hot with flames of anger shooting out of them and smoke coming out of his ears. The whistle blew. Crashes and checks everywhere. Where was the ball? Where was the ball?

HAWWWNK!

They had a goal.

Immediately Jake looked back and slammed his stick on the ground. He was swearing like Ralphie in *Christmas Story* when he finally took down the bully. (#$@#$@ %$%$ #%$^!, #$%$W%#$ #$%!#$!)

Not good.

Seconds later, another goal.

Jake got tossed for unsportsmanlike conduct.

Final score of the turkey shoot: 6–0.

The Field Sports staff went on to the finals. The title game went into overtime. After overtime left things unsettled, the game would be decided on penalty shots. Carvillak lined up with a chance to win the game, and he hit the first-ever penalty shot game winner to give his team the 1996 broomball title.

Now he had a title.

"I'm not talking about one title either. Not six, not seven…"

Actually, Lebron Carvillak was happy with his one title. And he let me know it.

"So, the Nature staff played well last night?"

"Dude, we lost to you guys six to zero."

"Well, I mean you played well for the Nature staff. The expectations weren't very high for you guys anyway. Have fun teaching kids how to spot chipmunk tracks in the wild."

AARRGGHH!

In 1997, I missed broomball because it didn't occur the one and only week I volunteered at camp. For the sake of building momentum, let's just say I failed to make the playoffs that year.

In 1998, I volunteered again but because I was a volunteer, I was asked to referee broomball. There's an emotional story. Guy can't win big game (any game), so he quits to ref. Not exactly *Hoosiers* right there.

In 1999, we had one more crack at broomball. Of all my goals that summer, wining a broomball title wasn't really on the list. I think the only thing on the broomball list was "please don't get embarrassed again."

But something interesting happened that summer. They changed the rules leading up to our broomball tournament.

No more wide open cross-checks, no more slamming into the boards, no more heart attacks. This time if it happened, you were ejected for the half on violation one, banned entirely on violation two. I guess the rules and infractions committee figured out that less contact meant fewer cardiac arrests and seizures. That rule change definitely worked for me and my staff of aspiring Dungeons and Dragons dicemasters. Right now, I bet there's a fat guy sitting at home in his Barcalounger who complains that the NFL is making it a league for girls when the new rules come out that favor the QB and the receiver; but I personally was tired of being the receiver of 6–0 asskickings.

We also had a different makeup for this year's team. Along with myself, we had the Cardellano brothers, Victor and Michael. Victor was a star fencer with ridiculous hand-eye coordination. He was also a bona fide hothead who melted down worse than Christian Bale on a movie set when he was angry. ("*OH, GOOD FOR YOU*!!!") Victor volunteered to be our goalie. We also had a couple of younger, fast guys on the team. Immediately I realized that for this to work, and for us to not get embarrassed for the sixth year in a row, we were changing our lineup. I firmly declared that I would stay back and not attack at all. I would help anchor the Mannerheim Line of broomball defense. Also we had two new players added to our team. They worked on a boat that was owned by a camp benefactor. We were being given two new players, both of whom actually knew how to play sports and conduct manual labor.

This was the tournament seeding for the 1999 camp broomball championship:

#1 : Director All-StarTeam: Number #2 : Waterfront

8: Scoutcraft #7: CITs

Champion__________

#4: Field Sports #3: Rangers

#5 NatureStaff #6 Handicraft

Here is a quick breakdown of the teams heading into broomball 1999, with each team being compared to its NCAA tournament counterpart.

#1 seed: Director All Stars

The camp director and some of the higher-ups who didn't work in a specific area had the ability to form their own team and get the best players they wantedfrom different areas or from parts of staff that didn't have a full team. For the sake of comparison, this collection of one-and-done wonders was the Kentucky Wildcats of the tournament.

#8 Seed: The Scoutcraft Area

The Scoutcraft area had one ridiculous bruiser of an athlete on their team named Preston. They also had the benefit of adding Ted from scuba. This gave them two solid athletes to build around. For the tournament's sake, they were the Navy led teams of the David Robinson era.

#4 Seed: Field Sports

A ton of athleticism and talent up and down the broomball court, but not as tough as you need to be come tournament time. Think of the Purdue Boilermakers here.

#5 Seed: The Nature Area

We had never won anything. Nor had we even come close. Fortunately, we didn't have to face the rangers or the Waterfront staff in the first round. Otherwise there were long odds on our team. Northwestern would be a suitable choice here.

Number three seed: Rangers

Athletic and aggressive. They swarmed all over you on defense and pushed the ball as fast as possible. The Memphis Tigers.

#6 Seed: Handicraft

Too undersized to be considered much of a tournament factor. Not enough depth either. Baylor Bears.

#2 seed: Waterfront

High seed and favorable draw guaranteed based on name alone. Elitist, blond hair, blue eyes. Get all the calls from the referees in their favor. Gentlemen, I give you the Duke Blue Devils.

#7 Seed: CITs

The counselors in training were all younger kids. They were mostly fifteen-year-olds who would get hired onto staff full-time. Also, they were freakishly athletic and taller/

stronger than 90 percent of the staff. Due to the fact their starters were all freshmen, we'll label them the Michigan Wolverines of the Fab Five Era.

In the opening round of play, we were actually first up to kick-off the tournament. Field Sports was a familiar opponent to us. That's because we had been their homecoming beatdown in 1996.

The whistle blew and the ball was live. I was amazed. We had fast wingmen on the point. Our defense was holding. The play was at their goal, not ours for once. Then I heard the magic whistle.

We scored a goal.

> "The shot heard 'round the world. The Nature staff displayed a modicum of athletic talent."

Our first goal ever as far as I knew. Our first lead ever. Could the game please end now? But it kept on going. We kept on striking forward. Whistle! Whistle again!

Finally, the ball was heading back to the defensive end, right in my neck of the woods and I took a big swing. You couldn't let your broom swing wildly. In theory, no broom bristle was allowed to go above waist height on a swing, otherwise you incurred a penalty. My swing was controlled. The broomball flew forward from our defensive neutral zone. It gained some momentum, hit a side table, and…

Goal!

Final score: NatureStaff-6-0.

We were advancing, baby!

This was the next round of play.

#8:Scoutcraft ___________

#5: Nature ___________

#7 CITs ___________

#3: Rangers ___________

It was upset city. Anybody's tournament. Dick Vitale couldn't hold back his excitement any longer. Then he remembered Duke lost and cried on camera for four straight hours.

In our second game we had to overcome Preston. He was an undersized tight end with a mean streak whenever he played competitive sports. Also, Ted from scuba would whine when he didn't like a call. I remembered this from when I was a referee the summer before. Everybody loves the amateur athlete that acts like he's Paul O'Neill on any call that goes against him.

Our little guys snuck forward.

Boom. Preston cross-checked one of them.

Penalty on Preston. This was awesome. One more and you're out. Penalty on Ted. Their two best players couldn't keep up.

We scored.

We scored again.

WE SCORED AGAIN.

3–0.

Then the comeback started.

They got a goal. Our goalie blew a gasket.

3–1.

They got another goal.

3–2.

Our goalie yelled at me to play defense instead of fucking around. Wasn't I his boss? No matter.

Now we were watching the clock. It was down to the final minutes. We were so close. If they scored, nobody on our wanted it to go to overtime.

Then a breakaway and one of our guys scored a goal.

4–2. Awesome. Our goalie still yelled and screamed, directing traffic like he was Peyton Manning at the line of scrimmage.

They scored again.

4–3.

They got the ball back. Seconds ticked by…

I raised my stick to swat down a ball.

The whistle blew. *FWWW!*

"High stick, Jaffe. Two minutes!"

I had to sit for an eternity.

Tick, tick, tick, tick, tick

Tick, tick, tick, tick, tick

My penalty was up. I was back out there. The buzzer sounded. Ballgame.

NatureStaff 4–3 winners!

Then we went outside. I turned to one of the guys on staff, Mitch.

"We're in the finals. We could win this thing."

All of a sudden a bunch of scouts started walking toward us on the dining hall porch. I knew why they were here. They were here to congratulate us. I was ready with my vast array of sports clichés.

> "Just taking it one game at a time. Gotta give credit to my teammates. If you kids stay in school, good things can happen. This game ball goes to my grand-momma who raised me like I was her own."

One of the scouts looked at me.

"Are you giving the star hike tonight?"

What? Huh? No fucking way. We we're about to play in the broomball finals and we had to go do a star hike so a bunch of snot-nosed little punk tenderfoots could get their astronomy merit badge? I didn't come to camp to help a bunch of Boy Scouts. I came to camp to win a broomball title. *It's not even a required merit badge, people.* I got my astronomy merit badge *after* I got my Eagle, for Christ's sake.

I gathered the Nature staff.

Time for the captain's speech before the big game.

"We need to go take these kids on their God damn star hike, and get their star tests completed ASAP so we can get back for the final game. Who's got the star hike tonight?"

"I do."

It was Corinne. Thank God. Our one girl on staff. We could leave her up there if we needed to.

Then Peterson chimed in: "I'll help her."

Mitch: "We should all help her. Then we can all get back faster."

What the hell was this nonsense! I wasn't looking for teamwork. I was looking to win the game and claim broom-ball glory in front of the Gods. OK, fine. Now that it's Camp Touchy-Feely, let's all go help each other.

We all raced up to the top of the hill to help the kids on their star tests.

"What's that star?"

"Big Dipper."

"Yep."

"What about that one?"

"Little Dipper."

"Good, good. And how's about that one over there?"

"Medium Dipper."

"Works for me. Let's go."

We passed those kids like we were in an inner city Chicago public school system that didn't want to lose its funding.

I'm pretty sure that if the Lakers were taking the bus to the arena before game 7 against the Celtics andthey saw a busload of abandoned orphans on the roadside who needed help, they wouldn't have to stop. It was totally unfair that we were inconvenienced by the Boy Scouts at the Boy Scout camp. But we sucked it up and did it anyway. God damn kids!

Now it was a race back to the dining room for the Finals.

After our sprint we all stopped to catch our breath, hoping we wouldn't be penalized for being late.

The game was stopped.

The CITs and the rangers were standing in the middle of the floor. Our camp director was talking to them.

> "Now look. If there's any more fighting, then broomball is cancelled permanently."

What the hell was this?

I turned to Clint.

> "What's going on?"
>
> "They got into two fights, and one of the CITs got hit by a broom in the eye. Camp director's pissed and he might call it."

Are you serious? They were gonna call off broomball? We were so close. All we had to do was beat one of the two teams that was infinitely more athletic and superior to us across the board. And it was about to be cancelled?

We almost killed a guy when this sport started. It wasn't cancelled back then.

Well that's super. I guess because Maximus and Commodus don't get along so well we can't re-create the fall of mighty Carthage.

The camp director looked everybody over. Both sides did an insincere, half-assed handshake. It wasn't much, but it was détente.

I turned to Mitch.

> "They've beaten the hell out of each other. This is emotional. We've got a really good chance here because they don't hate us."

It was true. The rangers and CITs had pranked each other, fought over girls, flipped each other's canoes and kayaks. Their grudge match was being settled now in the broomball arena of death. Two staffs enter. Only one leaves...

The game played on and the final whistle blew. The Rangers lost to the CITs.

Mitch turned to me.

> "You know, their goalie plays hockey. He's in a club at school *AND* he plays street hockey on the weekends."

Got it. Martin Brodeur is minding the pipes for them. Oh well.

THE TITLE GAME

#5: Nature Staff__________ ______________#7: CITs

CHAMPION __________

Because the previous game had been stopped more times than a Laker game during the hack-a-Shaq era, we now had a time constraint. The championship match would consist of two five-minute halves as opposed to ten minutes.

The CITs weren't physically tired at all. Far from it. They were, however, emotionally exhausted.

Works for me.

Thirty seconds in we got a lucky bounce and the ball whisked up, over, and past their goalie. Fluke play. Total fluke play.

This isn't pool. You don't need to call your shots. Fluke plays are welcome here.

We were up 1–0.

Vincent was screaming at us.

"Mind your side! Mind your side! Don't let them through!" The guy was red faced and shaking. Nice.

The first half ended.

We knew we weren't getting another goal. The other goalie was a brick wall after his one mental error.

We watched the clock tick. Then I decided to do something incredibly stupid. Monumentally stupid.

In the pantheons of coaching idiocy, this was conversation worthy. I wanted to put in Stevie.

If you want to know who Stevie is, go rent the movie *Lucas*. You could also watch what happens when Rudy goes up against the Notre Dame O-Lineman, or better yet, rent *Raging Bull* so you can see the mismatch that occurs between Jake Lamotta and the wife who undercooks his steak.

Stevie was in his first year on staff at our camp. He was an unusual kinda fella. During the summer, Stevie would literally be running under the dining hall at camp and decide to jump. This was all fine and good outside, but not inside a dining room with low ceiling beams. Stevie jumped straight up, hit his head, and fell down. Two seconds later he bounced back up and went running away as though nothing had happened. We had to warn Stevie against jumping in the dining hall since *THIS WASN'T THE FIRST TIME THIS HAD HAPPENED*. If he was diving into the water, he would hit his head on a cleat before he tasted the ocean. If he was slamming an A-frame door, he would forget to remove his forehead from the trajectory. *W*HACK!

Straight out of central casting, Stevie was our last guy on the bench. Stevie had barely played.

Overcome with guilt, I decided to put him in.

Kobe Bryant was coming out of game seven because Phil Jackson wanted Adam Morrison in the game so he could tell his parents…

We only had a minute to go. The clock was ticking.

Stevie was running around. He swung and missed. Yep, the top of his broom handle hit him in the stomach. He knocked the wind out of himself. Raise your hand if you knew that was coming.

Forty-five seconds…

Stevie, God bless him, was still out there, and Vincent had already made one kick save so that Stevie could be a part of the team.

Thirty seconds…

We cleared the ball and then it bounced right back. The CITs were coming for us like Genghis Khan, destroying everything in their path.

Shot on goal…

Wide right. Ricochet.

Fifteen seconds…

I turned to Corinne, who was also on the bench with me. (Hey, I'm not putting in Stevie *AND* the girl. Give me some credit here for strategy.)

Ten seconds…

We started to count down.

Five seconds…

"Four. Three. Two. One!"

The whistle blew. We were finally champions! Celebration at midfield.

There was a miniaturized champions cup that was ours for the taking. I grabbed it and said:

"Everyone gets a drink from the Stanley Cup. To the water fountain at once!"

The rest of the staff put away the tables and chairs from the arena. We would help them in due time. Well to be fair, my staff would. Me, not so much.

After six seasons we were champions. Sweet victory tasted like tap water—and it was glorious.

XVI

I Can't Believe I Missed the Boat Home!!!

The Five Most Controversial Campfire Skits I Ever Witnessed at Camp:

1.) "Men on Catalina"
A direct parody of the ingenious *In Living Color* sketch. This sketch was cut off the second one of the scouts said, "And then we went to the nature area where they showed us their big snake."
2.) "Birds of Prey"
One "Bird" (a senior staff member in a makeshift diaper, flapping his arms) chews up a bite of apple and gives it to the baby birds (younger staff in diapers, flapping their arms). Sometimes the baby birds would give the food back. Violates every major health code out there and has since been banned.
3.) "Smooth and Creamy"

A song in which the object was to cover the other person in shaving cream while singing the lyrics: "Smooth and creamy, we love smooth and creamy. Smooth and creamy, it's the game for me" (Not at all gay [cough, cough], but oh so much super fabulous fun. Thanks for asking.)

4.) "Home in LA"
A kid from my troop taught us this song, and we sang it at a campfire before I even worked on staff. It was a parody of "Home on the Range." I think this kid saw it on TV and took credit for the song like he wrote it. One of my favorite catchphrases was:
"Home, home in LA,
Where the bums get drunk all day.
The cops drag them in, and they get out again,
Oh give me a home in LA."

5.) "The O. J. Trial Skit"
One of my friends was an assistant scoutmaster back in 1995, and the kids from his troop did an O. J. trial reenactment that took place in the woods. It starred Marcia Lark and Christopher Bear Den.

If you wanted to get home from camp, there were not a lot of options. Being on an island meant that you had to find a boat home in order to get to the mainland. The one advantage we had was that we had a supply boat: the *Miss Christy*.

We even sang a song in her honor to the theme of the *Love Boat:*

"The *Christy.*

Soon she'll be making another run.

The *Christy...*

Working at scout camp is so much fun."

The *Christy* dropped off supplies a couple times a week. If you wanted a ride back, you just hopped on the *Christy* and had somebody pick you up when you arrived on the mainland. Easy enough.

This was the simplest way to get home. Otherwise you had to get a motorboat ride to the Isthmus, then wait for the cattle barge or the *Catalina Express* to take you home. Both those options cost money. Money was not an option.

I was leaving camp on a Friday. Normally you left camp on a Saturday because our day off was twenty-four hours from noon to noon, approximately. However, I was leaving a day early because "I had a personal and very serious family matter to attend to that weekend."

My family matter was that I had a small case of island fever coming on and needed more than one day to get away. If I left Friday afternoon and came back Sunday, then I could avoid burnout on the greatest job in the world, which was also the easiest job in all of camp. My detailed regimen of making sure kids passed geology merit badge while I drank lots of alcohol was wearing me down...almost like an igneous rock formation that was being broken down by wind and rain (Bud Light and fruity rum-flavored pirate drinks.). Besides, it was opening weekend for what I knew was going to be the greatest, most socially and culturally important movie of all time, *Independence Day*, and I loved me some Will Smith. ("Girl, look at his chest. He fine. He fine.")

The plan was falling into place. On Friday morning I was all packed up and ready to leave. Just for curiosity's sake, I checked around to see if anybody else was going to be on the *Christy* with me. Usually there was another person deadheading, just like Leonardo DiCaprio in *Catch Me if You Can.* Nobody on nature staff. Anybody else? Rangers, no; waterfront, no. But wait, "There was another."

Lara was going. Lara was a certified blond angel. She was our Swedish scuba instructor and she was magnificent.

(*Catch Me with Your Cans.*)

Our camp implemented a scuba program a few years before. Turns out scouts weren't content to just sit in geology merit badge and learn about the eroding sandstone outcrops of the Grand Canyon. (We could lose them, people! Don't you care?) One summer, I was even forced to audit a geology merit badge class that was taught by an actual high-school geology teacher. Oh, boy! (Kill me now.)

In 1994 or 1995, our camp decided to implement a scuba program. With a scuba program came scuba instructors. With the exception of a couple guys here and there, each and every scuba instructor was a stunning girl. My friend, Rory, personally went through more scuba instructors than thesharks in the movie *Open Water.* Davonte once woke me up at three in the morning because he could hear Rory having sex with a scuba instructor—on the other side of the hill!

In my first encounter with a scuba instructor, I was serving dessert in the kitchen when Caro, a six-foot-tall, dark-haired stunner, walked up to me.

("Of all the ice cream lines in all the world, she had to walk into mine.")

Caro turned to me and asked if she could have the ice cream that I was clasping with my suddenly nervous and sweaty kung fu grip.

I turned to her with this responseverbatim:

> "Uhm, uh heah, we uhm, have uh, ice uh, cream if uhm, like I uh, could uhm, give you uh, two ice creams and it uhm, would uhm, like I could do that for you."

Caro walked away without the ice cream, which I had now punctured with my thumb in sheer terror.

The second she left, Davonte jumped in back of me and reenacted my speech.

> "UHM, UHH, AAAHH! Dog, you are the biggest loser I know. You're a fucking Idiot."

That I was, that I was.

Lara the Swedish scuba Instructor was there in 1996. It was her only summer on staff. Turns out, she too was going home on the Friday afternoon *Christy.*

I had an isolation play. She was trapped on the *Christy* with me like she was Tallulah Bankhead in the the movie *LifeBoat.* I didn't need to push any Nazis into the water (which I was too much of a pussy to do anyway, as we've already established). It was just us. Not only was it just us, but I had a full hour on the boat to convince her to spend the weekend hanging out with me. This was perfect.

I was walking around camp like I owned the joint. It was getting close to lunchtime. I owned this. It was mine. In the bag. Nothing could possibly go wrong here.

The program director saw me.

> "Seth, would you mind helping us serve lunch? We need a few more servers."

All I had to do here was say the right thing. To clarify, I had to say the right thing in the right tone.

What I should have said:

"Geez, I would love to, but the *Christy* is leaving soon and, heh, is it OK if I help for five to ten minutes, and then if they don't need me I can race back down because it's really important I don't miss the *Christy* since I have a family event this weekend? I'm a team player and I just want to help out here. Is that OK?"

Again, that's the line of BS I should have fed the program director. What I actually said:

"Are you kidding me? Seriously! This is such bullshit! I have to get on the *Christy* so I can get the hell out of here this weekend, and now you want me to help? Come on, really?"

The program director made an executive decision right then and there. I would help serve lunch.

For those of you who hate it when bad things happen to bad people, I encourage you to stop reading this chapter right now.

I looked at the large clock in the dining hall. It read 11:30 a.m. The *Christy* was supposed to leave at 12:30 p.m. If I helped serve lunch and then just ran back, I would be fine. As long as the *Christy* didn't leave early.

I served with all the warmth and enthusiasm as the servers who worked at the dining hall my freshman year at the dorms.

> "Excuse me, sir," a scout would ask. "Can I have a bigger piece of cobbler?"
>
> "No, you can't. You're too fat."
>
> "Do scoutmasters get more french fries?"
>
> "Not if the doctor wants them to live past the age of fifty they don't."

The line receded. I was done. I dropped my serving attire and went running down to the docks.

My gear was already down there, so I was good. All I needed to do was grab my bag and hop on board.

This was perfect. The supply boat was about to send me home for an important family emergency that involved me watching the Fresh Prince of Bel Air terminate space aliens with extreme prejudice. Although, it was gonna' be hard to watch Will Smif cropdust all those evil terrestrials while I was busy making out with my new girlfriend.

"Yo, I have got to get me one of these."

I ran down to the dock like I was chasing after the French lieutenant's woman. Assuming she was a crazy hot Swedish scuba master.

That was weird. The *Christy* wasn't there. The boat must have done a lap around the bay to warm up the outboard motor silent-propulsion system. That made sense. I mean, the idea that they would leave without me, when I had such big plans, and love was in the air between me and Lara (the girl with no sagging flat boobs) was preposterous.

I turned to one of the unsuspecting kids on the waterfront staff.

Oh, this poor child. Time to launch a tomahawk missile at the messenger.

"Hey, do you know where the *Christy* is?"

"Uhm, Seth, I uh, think it left."

I turned red.

"What? Excuse me!"

The temperature on the kettle was starting to heat up a little bit more. I asked the waterfront director:

"Where's the *Christy*?"

The waterfront director didn't mind being the bearer of this news. It probably made his day.

"Oh, it's gone, Seth. It took off about fifteen minutes ago. Such a shame. You just missed it."

I could picture Vincent from *Pulp Fiction* telling Jules:

"I'm just saying, it's bad to rev a race car when it's in the motherfucking red. All right, that's all I'm saying."

One mission was on my mind.

Where was the program director?

I stomped from the waterfront across the parade ground. Furiously I was pacing. Where was the program director?

I didn't see him when I walked up to the dining hall. I walked around the back. Just outside of the back of the dining hall were a couple of benches. The servers ate there. There was also a small hill. The benches and the hill were in full range of the scouts eating lunch.

Word had already spread that I was angry. Time for my friends on staff to poke the bear at the zoo with a stick.

"Hey, Seth, what's up? Why are you still here?"

"Yeah, buddy. Didn't the *Christy* leave?"

"Weren't you supposed to be on it?"

Hhhmmm!!! Hhhmmm!!! Hhhmmm!!!

Boom!

I snapped. At that exact moment, all sanity left my brain. My perfect weekend with Lara ruined, the possibility of not seeing *Independence Day* and finding out if we really did fight back on the Fourth of July gone. I melted down worse than the stock market during a margin call.

> "I can't believe I missed the *Christy*! I can't believe I missed the boat home!"

I yelled it again, only louder this time.

"I CAN'T BELIEVE I MISSED THE *CHRISTY*!!! I CAN'T BELIEVE I MISSED THE BOAT HOME!"

The head cook, God bless her heart for asking, tried to console me.

> "Well, Seth, why are you so mad? You can get another boat back home, I'm sure."
>
> "IT DOESN'T MATTER. NOTHING MATTERS. IT'S NOT FAIR. I HELPED SERVE THE SCOUTS THEIR STUPID MEAL AND NOW HERE I AM AND I CAN'T BELIEVE I MISSED THE *CHRISTY*. I CAN'T BELIEVE I MISSED THE BOAT HOME!"

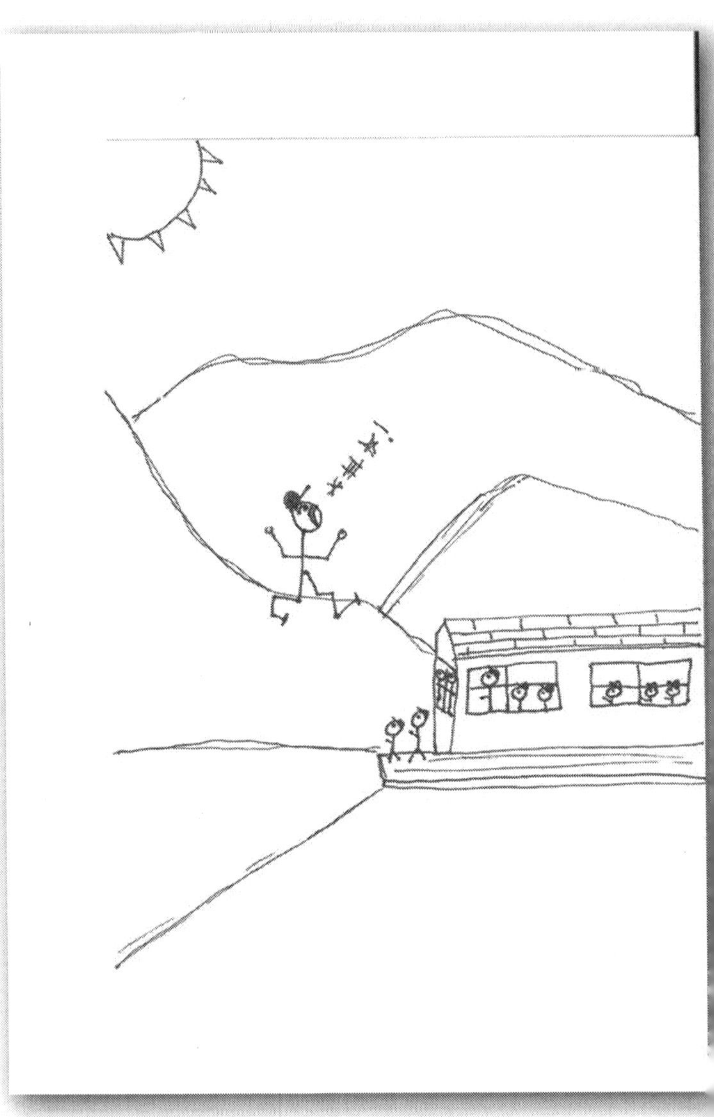

A kid named Ralph happened to be in the dining hall when I went full-on angry in front of everybody. Years later, he told me about how scared he was at the time as he watched me melt down like Charlie Sheen on a publicity tour. He wasn't even on staff at the time. He was one of the scouts in the dining hall.

After about ten minutes of me storming up and down the hill, the program director found me.

Not good.

"Walk with me, Seth."

He didn't yell it. He didn't scream it. He just said it, and it worked.

I followed him, and now I was quiet. Still raging, but very quiet.

He marched me into the business office.

"Sit down."

"Fine!"

My arms were crossed and I was looking straight down. My temper tantrum extraordinaire had gone on for a solid thirty minutes.

"Seth, I'm sorry you missed your boat." Now he raised his voice. "IT DOES NOT, HOWEVER, GIVE YOU AN EXCUSE TO MARCH AROUND AND THROW A FIT LIKE YOU'RE AN INFANT CHILD."

"I helped serve a meal. I didn't even need to be there. And I missed the boat home."

(I deserved to act like a child, people.)

"Seth, there are other boats home. Somebody can take you to the Isthmus and you can get a boat from there. Why was this boat such a big deal anyway?"

(Because I value the one-in-a-million chance I thought I had of getting laid more than I value feeding these whiny, Totin'-Chip-ruining, Baden-Powell retreads. Especially when they're just going to end up at the trading post anyway jamming their faces full of Junior Mints and Rootbeer Suicides.)

I opted to table that speech for a later day.

"You're right. I didn't need to take this boat."

My shoulders slumped. The pressure at failing to score with women was gone. With no shot to score with the scuba girl I could feel the stress drain away from my body, and it was enlightening.

"I can take another boat later."

The next week I was down at the docks helping to unload the supply boat. The nice thing about working with my peer group was that they would feel sorry for me. They wouldn't use my pain and sorrow to mock me. My personal loss did not constitute a chance for exploitation.

(Never show the enemy any weakness whatsoever.)

The *Christy* turned the corner toward camp.

As if on cue, I heard Allen and Clint chime in:

"OK, everybody. On the count of three."

Collectively: "ONE! TWO! THREE!"

A small army of camp staff started stomping around and yelling, "I CAN'T BELIEVE I MISSED THE *CHRISTY*! I CAN'T BELIEVE I MISSED THE *BOAT HOME*!"

They looked like the cavemen in the beginning scene of the movie *2001*.

But at least this wouldn't become a landmark moment in my career at the Boy Scout camp. I mean, I wouldn't be defined by this singular gesture of over-the-top rage, would I?

Three years later I came back for the full summer on staff. During the first day of setting up camp, we took time to bond as areas. I met the nature staff. For the first time they met me as a director. We were all asked as part of a team-building exercise to conduct a small staff skit that illustrated the importance of safety in camp.

Skit number one was performed by the waterfront staff and illustrated the importance of always wearing a life preserver.

Cue the horrible overacting that could be found in any Uwe Boll movie:

Enter waterfront staffman number one.

"I'm a scout, and I can go out on any boat I want to without wearing a life preserver because I just don't care about safety."

Enter waterfront staffman number two.

"No, you can't. I know you can't because my name is Seth Jaffe, and I'm on staff here. I always wear a life preserver, especially when I'm on the *Christy*. And what's that you say? I missed the *Christy*? That can't be right.

"I CAN'T BELIEVE I MISSED THE *CHRISTY!* I CAN'T BELIEVE I MISSED THE *BOAT HOME*!"

End scene.

Skit number two was performed by the rangers.

It featured an in-depth, dramatic look at the dangers of running in camp.

Cue the next Oscar-worthy scene:

Enter rangers one and two.

Ranger number one: "Camp safety is so important."

Ranger number two: "I know and, *hey*! Why are those scouts running?"

Enter rangers dressed as running scouts about to get a lecture on immoral running behavior.

Ranger number one: "Don't you kids know it's wrong to run in camp? You could fall and hurt yourselves. Why were you in such a hurry anyway?"

Oh boy, here we go again.

Scouts collectively: "Because we didn't want to miss the *Christy*. We can't believe we forgot about the *Christy*! We can't believe we forgot about the boat home*!*"

At least get your lines right if you're gonna do it. What the hell was this, amateur hour?

Skit number three was our responsibility. After debating with my staff, I decided we needed to do a public service announcement about the dangers of scouts bringing spear guns into camp and shooting them at each other. It was revolutionary work in its own right. Not to overhype my acting chops here, but you could call our skit "Casablanca II."

Shakespearean actors, places please.

And action:

Nature staff actor number one: "Oh boy. I have this spear gun in camp. I can have so much fun. Whatever shall I do?"

Nature staff actor number two, nowhere near on cue: "Hey, guys, what's that? No wait, be careful."

A fake spear air gun launched it's hurling invisible projectile. Our second actor fell to the ground like he was Sir Laurence Olivier in *Hamlet.*

At which point I entered with my concluding speech.

> "You guys can't bring spear guns into camp.
>
> "I can't believe you guys brought weapons into camp.
>
> "I can't believe you're all taking part in drive-by spear gun shootings.
>
> *"AND MOST IMPORTANT:*
>
> "I can't believe...I can't believe...I can't believe I..."

(Let's see Sir Laurence Olivier deliver his lines in between raucous bouts of laughter.) missed the *Christy!*"

XVII

The Last Barge Dinner

Five Worst Foods I Ever Ate at Boy Scout Camp:

1.) Roast beef bologna slice served on top of mashed potatoes with gravy, affectionately known as donkey-dick (mmm-mmm)
2.) Dehydrated turkey tetrazzini (just add water, then it will taste good)
3.) A dirty head of lettuce (served the first year you could get a vegetarian option)
4.) Half-frozenBlack bean burgers (served the second year you could get a vegetarian option)
5.) Sloppy Joes

The year 1996 was not my last year on staff. Far from it. I volunteered for a week in 1997 as well as in 1998.

In 1999, I returned for the whole summer.

However, 1996 was the end of an iconic moment, not just for me but for the camp as well. It was the last barge dinner. For years, the directors had had an end-of-the-summer dinner. We reminisced about everything and everyone in camp. We did this while never acknowledging that the real world was awaiting us. Instead we chose to enjoy the moment. In my first summer on staff, the directors took a cruise to Avalon, the big city on Catalina Island. When they got back into camp, they weren't just happy. They were quiet. Their happiness was hidden amid a line of smug grins. I knew right then and there that I needed to get invited to one of those dinners. By 1995, the dinner was no longer a cruise. It was held instead on a barge that was normally reserved for storing kids' luggage when they arrived and subsequently left camp.

In 1995, I was still not a director. At the end of the summer, I could literally look out at the directors having fun on their barge dinner. Being the veteran on staff who wasn't invited to the directors' dinner meant I commanded as much respect as the high-school senior who was held back twice, or the veteran on the minor league baseball team with the most tenure. Well, God damn, it was about time for Crash Davis to get his call up to 'The Show.'

In 1996 I was finally eligible. I put my name in the draft, hired an agent, and was officially a certified pro director. I even did time at camp school to get ready for this momentous event. The end of summer was finally approaching. As August wound down, a date was selected for our barge dinner.

During the day, I tried not to think about it. This would be the last time the directors would be alone for the summer as comrades. Earlier in the day, I went by the barge in a motorboat and looked at the setup. I wasn't manly enough to drive there on my own in a motorboat, so I had one of the junior staff take me. There was a giant grill on the barge as well as two tables and chairs. The setup was innocuous enough. It actually looked simple and pleasant. I believe they call this the calm before the storm. If that's the case, then nobody knew what to expect before Hurricane Cabernet Snapple Margarita aka Cabersnapplerita arrived.

We showed up for evening colors in camp. Colors started at 6:00 p.m., and if I knew one thing, the worst thing I could possibly do here was act stupid or show up late. Well, by God, if colors started at 6:00 p.m. sharp, then I knew full well that early was on time and on time was late. I was going to be early for once, God damn it! (6:07, not bad.)

Also, I didn't mouth off or make any smartass remarks. Instead, after the flags were taken down, I walked with Clint and Davonte's older brother to the boat that was taking us to the barge. I didn't even run because I didn't want to draw any attention to myself.

When we arrived, Davis was there. Davis was a resident camp benefactor. He showed up several times throughout the summer to help with anything from campfire skits to morale boosting. He had the grill working like he was Bobby Flay. There were quesadillas on the left side; on the right side there was a giant piece of foil. I had heard about this. Davis had a specialty. He knew how to cook salmon on a grill. "Come here, Seth. Put your hand down. Once it starts to sizzle you'll know it's good and ready." Again, this was a really nice and thoughtful dinner. Very well put together.

It was missing something.

To the right of the grill was the bar setup.

That something was drinks.

I was bartending tonight. For the first time ever, I would not only bartend, but I would mix the drinks.

Time to survey our options.

Red Wine—Check.

Snapple—Check.

Tequila—Check.

Good enough for me.

I slammed down a bottle of delicious ice cold Snapple. I did this because, first and foremost, it was fucking awesome. Second, I needed an empty bottle to mix my ingredients.

Ingredients:

½ bottle Snapple.

One shot tequila.

Red wine.

Reattach cap.

Shake vigorously.

Add one ice cube (ice cube optional).

Serve in classy red solo cup.

Navinson was my first patron of the evening. He was going into the army shortly. Ironically, he had never really drunk before tonight.

"Here you go, buddy. Down the hatch and through the snatch."

I don't believe he ever drank again after that night.

Like Tom Cruise in *Cocktail,* I effortlessly mixed magical beverages.

Next up was Clint.

"Enjoy, amigo. It's a Pink Lemonade Merlot Meritage with a small Cuervo twister on the backside."

Bartending was easy. I could do this forever. Not bad for somebody with no experience whatsoever mixing drinks. Could you tell?

Up next: The Compassion Berry Cabernet Sauvignon Surprise.

I kicked ass at bartending.

"For goodness' sake, I got the hippy hippy shake."

No way this would come back to bite us in the ass.

The camp director got up to make a speech.

He thanked us for our service as directors that summer. He told us how much it meant to him as a new director to have this support. He stressed our caring, compassion, and *Whoosh*!

I looked up.

Whoosh! Whoosh!

The junior staff were water ballooning us. They were using a funnelator (fancy scouting term for a water balloon launcher for all you civilians out there). Those little SOBs were lobbing aquatic bombs at us like we lived in an Israeli border town.

I watched the junior staff defy the Gods by pranking the entire director staff at our final director dinner. Endlessly they launched water balloons at us. They even had an inside man in their operation. It was my roommate Jonathan. He was Crash Davis this year. I had to hand it to him. Launching water balloons at us and exploiting child labor in the process—pretty awesome.

Whoosh! Whoosh! Whoosh!

I couldn't have been more proud of the junior staff than I was at that moment.

(Every one of them would suffer so much when I got back.)

Three directors left on a motorboat to halt the rebel insurrection. Water ballooning stopped shortly thereafter.

The night went on. Snapple mix drinks were a smashed success. The sun went down and we were now underneath a majestic army of stars. The salmon was ready. Dinner was served and immediately devoured. Davonte's older brother turned on the radio. It was *Club MTV Dance Party Time.* But first Clint grabbed me.

"I gotta pee, Jaffe. Help me out."

"Uhm yeah, Clint. Our friendship has boundaries and I don't…"

"Just hold the back of my shirt while I pee off the barge, Jaffe."

"Oh, OK. I can do that."

Clint was so obliterated on cocktails I had to hold the back of his shirt while he peed. I was boozed up as well. Clint was being held at a 45-degree angle over the barge while he peed straight down. For once in my life, I was forcing myself not to throw somebody in the water. Slowly I pulled him back up. On my watch, there was no way that Clint was going in the drink. In fact, it was my life's mission that night to make sure my buddy didn't fall into the water under any circumstances.

> "Conga line!" The program director yelled at the top of his lungs. We didn't blink. The man said conga line and he meant business. We all got in a line. The conga line was operating within a small square box that was surrounded by water. All you had to do was keep turning right and you were good to go.

First guy goes right. Second. Third. Hell, even I went right. It was Clint's turn. The man had been a high school track star. A superior athlete. His hand eye–coordination was far superior to…

SPLASH!

Instead of going right, Clint made a straight. He went right into the drink, doing his best Natalie Wood impression.

Two seconds later, Davonte's older brother, showing off for one of the women on staff, jumped in after Clint, without any clothing. "Man down, repeat: man down. Now bare-assed man is chasing man down!"

I made eyes at Lara. Our scuba instructor, my eternal flame, was still at camp, and I had one last dinner to woo her. I jumped up on a table and started rocking out to the song "Green-Eyed Lady."

"Pretty lady, green-eyed lady…"
"Hey, Lara, do you want to come up on the table and dance with me?"

(Worst intro line ever: inviting a girl to join a guy who's table dancing.)

"Lovely lady strolling slowly…"

CRASH! The table snapped in two.

Clint, who was now freshly soaked and out of the water, yelled:

"Ladies and gentlemen, Seth Jaffe is in camp."

Lara took two steps away.

Me Breaking Table
"Naked Guy"
Falling Guy
Aaargh

A shore boat approached next. It was Jimmy Walker. He was here to take us out to sea on a fun little cruise.

Jimmy Walker was a shore boat driver at Catalina. This was a guy who had lived a thousand lives before he ever set foot on camp. Police officer, stuntman, city councilman. The man was a living, breathing incarnation of John Wayne in my eyes. Hell, the man died at age seventy riding his Harley-Davidson to Utah. Lawrence of Arabia was a piker. Jimmy and a bare-assed Davonte's older brother unhitched our barge. We were moving. Yep, we were definitely moving.

Having watched the Nature Channel once in between loading up different VHS cassettes of *Vivid Video Starlets*, I knew something about the rigors of the wild. Jimmy Walker, the ultimate badass, was taking us out to sea like young braves who had to return as full-grown warriors.

I waited for him to yell at us to jump into the ocean with specific instructions not to emerge for air until we had killed a shark with our bare hands. I also knew that if it was a thresher and not a mako that Jimmy would be pissed. I wondered how much pussy I would get with my new sharktooth necklace. The one I would steal from Clint or Allen. I wasn't going in the ocean. After all, it was salty from all that whale sperm, right, Snookie?

Jimmy took our barge out into the water. We floated around lazily for a few more hours of drinking and dancing. We listened to the Guess Who, Van Morrison, and anything else that constituted our soundtrack of the summer of 1996. When Jimmy finally returned us to our mooring, we were absolutely exhausted. It was time to go to bed. Well, to be fair, most of us were sick and it was time to throw up the diabetes-inducing beverages I served all night long.

We loaded onto the motorboats and then I remembered one thing:

Payback!

The junior staff had dared to defy the Director Gods by catapulting water balloons in our direction. I swore on Zeus's honor they would be made to suffer. (Fair to say I had a small ego problem that summer.)

The junior staffers were asleep. But not for long. First thing I did was wake up my roommate Jonathan.

I did this because Jonathan was in on the hit. He wasn't a director and I had baited him all day long about being too much of a pussy to launch water balloons at the directors dinner. I couldn't help but feel no responsibility or accountability whatsoever in this situation. (Leadership!)

With little to go on and a hangover approaching fast on the horizon, I grabbed my athlete's foot spray.

"Hey, Jonathan, are you a bug?"

To be fair, I didn't spray him. I just sprayed in his vicinity. Chemical weapons don't have to be dropped directly on ground zero. Just deploy them nearby and wait for the wind to do its job.

After a few rounds of exterminating Jonathan with tough-actin' Tinactin, it was time to turn him to my side to vanquish the junior staff uprising.

"Jaffe, what the fuck are you doing? I'm not a fucking bug, Jaffe. What's wrong with you?"

"Look, Jonathan," I said as he held my drunk body up so I didn't fall over. "Forget about what you did. The important thing is I forgive you. Now we need to teach the junior staff a lesson."

It was time for something special: a pillow-beating party.

Now it was go time. This meant you grabbed your pillow and ceremoniously went around and threw some goosedown haymakers at the junior staff. This was a great idea. There were only a couple of logistical problems:

A.) Director sobriety;
B.) We were considerably outnumbered; and
C.) They were younger, hungrier, and faster.

I surveyed the losing scenario. Well, by God, if Davy Crockett and Yosemite Sam didn't surrender in Oklahoma at the Alamo, then we weren't surrendering either.

"Gentlemen, it's go time."

Earlier in the summer we launched a pillow-beating party, and while we were giving one kid on staff a few pillow tattoos, he grabbed his mattress and barreled over four of the directors like he was leading a Spartan phalanx formation. We high-fived the kid for his amazing efforts because we were so proud of him. Then we proceeded to Tempur-Pedic him into submission.

It became bedlam fast. The entire North Hill running around on a nihilistic pillow-beating jihad.

> "Death to the director infidels who launch a holy pillow-beating party on Catalinistan. Alalalalala!!!!!"

Whack Whack Whack!

The directors were getting overrun by the Apache nation, just like at the Alamo in Colorado.

We needed UN peacekeepers to come in and save our asses.

Just then the program director showed up. He had been on the opposite hill and had heard all our noise.

He centered himself on our hill nowas he got ready to yell. Oh well, at least since everybody was acting like a loon, I wouldn't get singled out.

> "Seth Jaffe! Enough is enough! You and the directors stop this now and leave the junior staff alone. Also, all junior staff need to go to bed now."

If you cut off the head of the beast, the body dies.

XVIII

Conclusion

5 Summer Camps We'd all go to as Adults

*List provided by Alexa Lyons at coed.com

1.) Camp Grounded Anderson Valley, CA
2.) Space Camp
3.) Rock 'n' Roll Fantasy Camp
4.) Wine Camp
5.) Wanderlust Yoga Festivals

Years ago, before I became a father, I read a book by Mitch Albom called *For One More Day*. The concept was very interesting: a man gets to go back in time and live out one day of his life.

I turned to my wife and askedher, "OK, honey, if you could go back in time and relive one day of your life, what day would it be?"

She didn't even pause. She looked over and said, "Oh, I think it would be wine tasting with you in Sonoma. That would be a good day." Then she turned to me and asked, "What about you?"

I paused and stuttered. "Well, uhm, it would be, uhm, wine tasting as well. Yeah, that's fun."

My wife looked me over and laughed. "Why don't you just admit that you would go back to Emerald Bay if you had one more day?"

She was absolutely right.

When I was at Emerald Bay, I felt like Peter Pan in Neverland. You knew there was a real world out there, but you just didn't care. Between campfires, pranks, and drinking with my best friends in the world, we lived in the moment. It was an amazing experience for us that remains permanently stitched in time.

When I see my friends from camp now, over twenty years after my first summer on staff, all we want to do is talk about camp. Our wives and girlfriends have heard these stories twenty times before. My wife will even say in her best *American Pie* voice:

"This one time at Boy Scout camp…"

It gets a good laugh.

Every experience, every moment. I was the luckiest person in the world because I worked at Emerald Bay. I look back at that amazing time in my life, and I don't have a single regret. All those guys I worked with—Carvillak, Nilius, Clint, Allen, Davonte, McBrayer, and everybody else—those guys are my brothers. When I look back at my time at summer camp, there's nothing I would have ever done differently. . . although it would have been nice if I could have had a threesome with Kailey and Lara.

The End

Our 1996 directors photo.
*The great thing about this picture is that this is the first time in history that it's been done.
(I'm next to Jesus).

When you write a book you need both a staggering amount of effort as well as relentless enthusiasm. There is a support team in place that made this book possible, and they deserve to be thanked for all of their efforts.

To my universe, Valerie and Nicholas. I couldn't have done this book without your support and I am forever grateful. Valerie your illustrations were perfect in reflecting what it's like to be a kid at Boy Scout Camp. Also, thank you for taking our baby all those times where I was writing. It was a Herculean effort and I can literally tell you this book doesn't' get done without you doing the heavy lifting. Nicholas, I can't wait for you to be old enough to have your adventures at summer camp. Thank you both again. I love you more than you know.

To my parents, thank you for everything. Dad, you are my mentor and my best friend and for that I am eternally grateful. I love you dearly. Mom, you are amazing and I love you as well.

Aaron Bleich, thank you for your first round of editing on this book. I needed some guidance in the beginning and you were there for me. Much appreciated buddy.

George and Brad at the Heckler. Thanks for allowing me to write for you guys, and for all the advice on getting published. Also, thanks for posting my articles. I'll be there next year to celebrate, when the curse is lifted, and the Chicago Fire finally have their coveted MLS title.

To the team at Createspace, thank you all for showing endless patience with somebody who truly had no idea what he was doing.

To my sister Becky Jaffe, someday I suspect you have a book in you and it probably will be a whole lot more intelligent and important that the one you have just finished reading.

Dan Bredeson, thanks for being a creative soundboard. Also, thanks for giving me a title. If it wasn't for you, my audience would have just finished reading *50 Shades of Boy Scout Camp.*

Joe Buzzello, thanks for giving me a blueprint. This book was sitting on my desk going nowhere until you told me what steps I needed to take next.

Annie Strenk, thanks for believing in me and reminding me that I needed to get this done. Your kick in the pants was well-timed.

I would also like to thank the following people for their efforts and support:

Victor and Esther Vega, Lee Harrison, Jon Riley, Nick and East Phillips, Dr Norman, Adam Michaels, David Pepin, Andrew Wilder, Josephine Roberts, David McAlister, Kai Hand, Terrie Hudson, Anna Reed, Jenny Cornet and Steven Cornet.

Lastly, my Scoutmaster Irwin Buck Friedman passed away just before this book was published. Buck, you were a great Scoutmaster and an even better man. You are missed dearly. I know you're up in heaven right now keeping tabs on us, as well as watching over your tent as it swings in the branches above Sespe Creek.

Made in the USA
San Bernardino, CA
04 August 2015